2015 design annual

Published by ORO Editions
Architecture, Art, and Design
Gordon Goff: Publisher
www.oroeditions.com
info@oroeditions.com

10 9 8 7 6 5 4 3 2 1 First Editions
ISBN: 978-1-941806-96-8

Proofreader: Sonya Mann
Production Manager: Usana Shadday

Color Separations and Printing: ORO Group Ltd.
Printed in China

DEDICATION

THIS BOOK IS DEDICATED TO ALL OF OUR WONDERFUL CLIENTS OVER THE PAST 60 YEARS. THANK YOU FOR SHARING YOUR DREAMS AND ASPIRATIONS AND FOR COLLABORATING WITH US TO CREATE EXTRAORDINARY PLACES.

PREFACE

This year marks HOK's 60th anniversary. George Hellmuth, Gyo Obata and George Kassabaum came from different backgrounds and perspectives. Yet our three founders shared a passion for designing exceptional spaces and places for people. They also had an ambitious vision for establishing a diverse, enduring design practice.

During our first 20 years, between 1955 and 1975, HOK's projects embodied our founders' design philosophy of creating functional yet beautifully expressive buildings that respond to people's needs.

By the 1970s, our reputation for designing single buildings with refined concepts and robust details began leading to significant commissions involving large-scale planning, landscape architecture and interior design. Diversity remained a fundamental theme, with large and small projects designed and detailed in accordance with unique functional and client requirements.

From 1976 to 1995, HOK expanded beyond the US to become an international design practice skilled in adapting to distinct climates and contexts around the world. From the deserts of the Middle East to the rainforests of Indonesia, we explored the potential of every project.

By the mid-1990s, HOK had two dozen offices working together to design interior spaces, buildings, communities and cities across the world. Our multidisciplinary approach to all building types helped establish a legacy of innovative, collaborative design solutions.

In 2015, 60 years after our founding, HOK's specialist expertise and geographic reach extend to nearly every building type and continent. Sustainability, technical advancement, creativity and practical innovation are hallmarks of our work. Each new design reflects our meticulous attention to the needs of the community and the natural environment.

Throughout our history, HOK has had the privilege of designing the building blocks that come together to form communities, improve cities and enhance people's lives. This book highlights recent examples.

Our 2015 Design Annual presents innovative corporate workplaces, enduring government buildings and a community-focused museum. We review several healthcare and science facilities — critical buildings in which clinicians and researchers are discovering new ways to improve lives. We examine the design of hospitality projects that create destinations for luxury and relaxation in exceptional settings. We look at futuristic sports venues, dynamic retail centers and sustainable residential environments. Finally, we feature several new expressions for airports and all forms of transit.

After six decades, the timeless architectural values of function, structure, light and beauty in service to human needs remain our guiding principles. We look forward to working with clients to create new memories and places over the next 60 years.

HOK Design Board

TABLE OF CONTENTS

PROJECT LOCATIONS

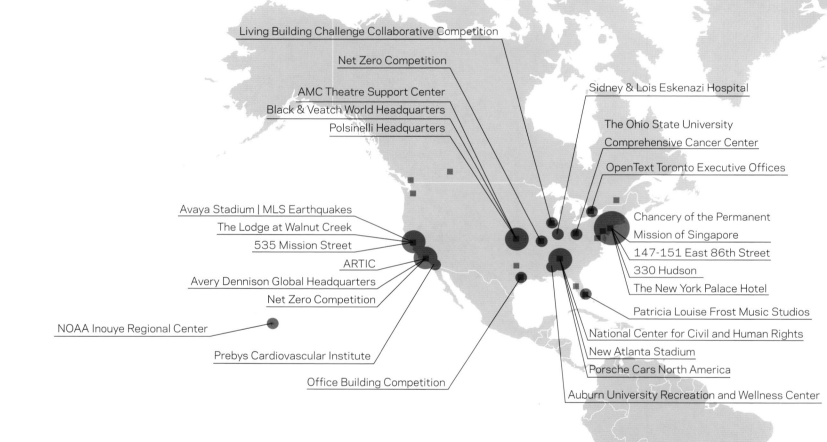

Living Building Challenge Collaborative Competition

Net Zero Competition

AMC Theatre Support Center
Black & Veatch World Headquarters
Polsinelli Headquarters

Sidney & Lois Eskenazi Hospital

The Ohio State University
Comprehensive Cancer Center

OpenText Toronto Executive Offices

Avaya Stadium | MLS Earthquakes
The Lodge at Walnut Creek
535 Mission Street
ARTIC
Avery Dennison Global Headquarters
Net Zero Competition

Chancery of the Permanent
Mission of Singapore
147-151 East 86th Street
330 Hudson
The New York Palace Hotel

NOAA Inouye Regional Center

Prebys Cardiovascular Institute

Office Building Competition

Patricia Louise Frost Music Studios

National Center for Civil and Human Rights

New Atlanta Stadium

Porsche Cars North America

Auburn University Recreation and Wellness Center

● HOK 2015 Design Annual Projects
■ HOK Office

Fitzrovia Apartments
The Francis Crick Institute
St Bartholomew's Hospital

NEF Ataköy 22 Mixed-Use Development

Hana Dream Town

Net Zero Competition

Hamad International Airport
Passenger Terminal Complex

Basrah Sports City

Tower Competition

Aramed Medical Village
Residential Community for
Confidential Corporate Client

Hospital Design Competition
Net Zero Competition
Suzhou Times Square
Suzhou Wujiang East Taihu Lake
Golden Bay Tourism Complex

Kempegowda International Airport,
Bengaluru Terminal 1 Expansion

Huafa New Town, Phase 6

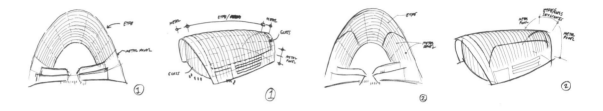

Anaheim Regional Transportation Intermodal Center

Anaheim, California, USA

67,000 sq. ft. / 6,225 sq. m.

Completion: 2014

The Anaheim Regional Transportation Intermodal Center (ARTIC) sets a precedent for civic-minded transit hubs in the US. HOK and Parsons Brinckerhoff designed ARTIC as an innovative new transit station that serves as a destination in itself. The project brings together transit, dining, retail and entertainment options in an iconic terminal building.

The transit hub links commuter and regional rail service and intercity bus systems including Amtrak, Metrolink, OCTA bus service and Anaheim Resort Transportation. ARTIC's flexible design ensures that it can serve as a southern terminus for California's future high-speed rail system.

Officials challenged the team to create an icon that would welcome a new age of public transportation. The station was also conceived as a catalyst for transforming Anaheim's core into a pedestrian-friendly zone that promotes connectivity. Known as the "Platinum Triangle," the area around the station includes Angel Stadium, the Honda Center, the Anaheim

Convention Center and Disneyland. The master plan establishes a clear pedestrian pathway flanked by future mixed-use development with ARTIC as the primary destination. The extroverted building has a significant but welcoming presence and will help spur transit-oriented development.

Drawing inspiration from classic grand transit halls including Grand Central Terminal in New York, along with the structural elegance of local airship hangars, the team developed a 21st-century design concept. The design achieves its signature parabolic form by employing a diagrid structural system of diamond-shaped steel arches infilled with translucent ETFE (ethylene tetrafluoroethylene) pillows. At the north and south ends, freestanding curtain walls bring in daylight and offer expansive views. The long-span, grid shell structure creates a grand, light-filled atrium space that accommodates open circulation.

The team used building information modeling (BIM) to develop ARTIC's complex form,

geometry and functions. BIM helped the team navigate the building systems and study the building's tolerances and environmental performance.

ARTIC is designed for LEED Platinum certification. The vault-shaped structure acts in concert with advanced mechanical systems to optimize energy efficiency. Inflated ETFE cushions cast a soft, translucent light throughout the great hall, while the additional frit pattern on the outer layer reduces solar heat gain. Convection currents naturally ventilate the building as heat rises from the lower south end up to the north side and out through operable louvers. The radiant heating and cooling floor system and optimized HVAC system will help reduce ARTIC's energy consumption by 50 percent.

LED lights mounted on the diagrid structure illuminate the ETFE pillows in gradations of shifting colors, providing a striking presence on the night skyline. As darkness falls, ARTIC becomes lit from within and acts as a beacon from the freeways and local streets.

◀ north entrance from plaza

▶ site plan

1 grand hall
2 retail
3 ticketing +
   information
4 support
5 service yard

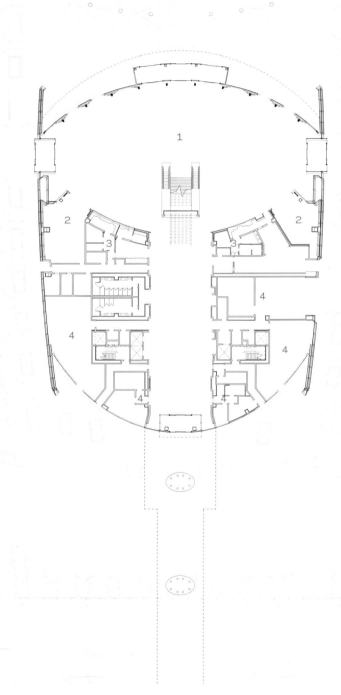

▲ view looking north from level 2

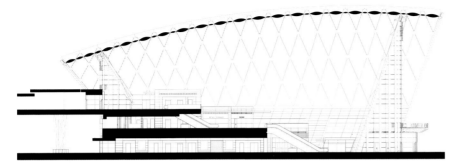

▲ north-south building section

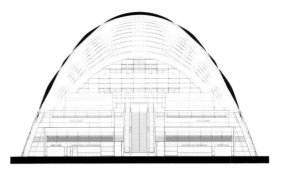

▲ east-west building section

▲ grand hall from north vestibule

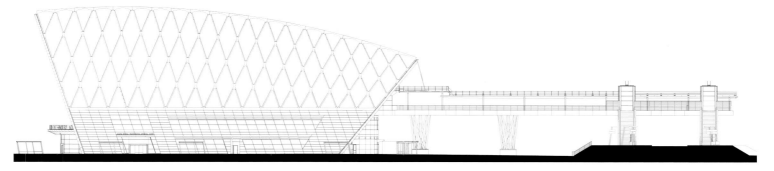

▲ west elevation

▲ view across grand hall

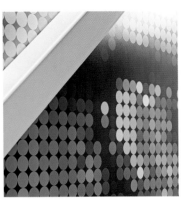  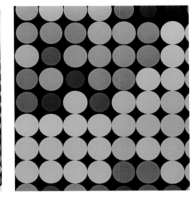

AMC Theatre Support Center
Leawood, Kansas, USA

120,000 sq. ft. / 11,150 sq. m.

Completion: 2013

AMC's Theatre Support Center celebrates the company's iconic brand and mission of creating an amazing movie-going experience.

Previously located in a nondescript downtown Kansas City office building that segregated staff across multiple floors, AMC wanted its new headquarters, which is part of the mixed-use Park Place development, to catalyze cultural change and celebrate the company's role in the entertainment industry. The open office floor plan breaks down barriers and enhances communication.

Wrapping most of the facade in glass enables daylight to permeate through the open interiors. Outdoor terraces with proportions mimicking the dimensions of a movie screen are part of all three visible building elevations.

As the building's cultural and functional centerpiece, a central stairway system communicates AMC's vision and values. It doubles as an office gathering space and multilevel theater, with digital media walls that stream news and the latest movie trailers from Hollywood.

Supported by a wide range of meeting spaces, the office accommodates individual work and team collaboration. More than 17,000 square feet of whiteboard surfaces offer a backdrop for continuous brainstorming and idea sharing.

A graphic history wall spotlights the story of AMC's growth, while bold splashes of red reinforce its brand. Design elements such as movie-inspired graphics and an exterior glass pattern inspired by the vertical folds of a movie curtain reinforce the company's industry leadership.

◄ building entrance

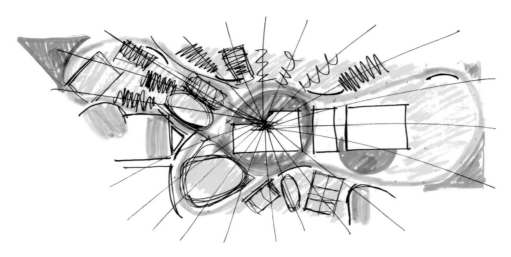

▲ concept sketch

▲ entrance lobby + history wall

▲ central stair + open office

▲ entrance + parking structure

▲ outdoor terrace

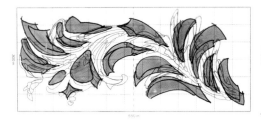  

Aramed Medical Village Development
Jeddah, Riyadh and Eastern Province, Saudi Arabia

Each village site:
18 million sq. ft. / 1.7 million sq. m.
418 acres / 169 hectares

Competition: 2014

This concept for three medical villages in key Saudi Arabian cities establishes a healthcare delivery channel that provides a more human-scaled, town-like environment than found in the larger medical cities under development by the Ministry of Health. The design creates a distinct prototype rooted in the spirit of integrated clinical knowledge development and care delivery.

Each medical village includes a 200-bed general hospital, a 200-bed specialty hospital and several collaborative clinical education buildings, including schools of medicine, dentistry, nursing, pharmacy and hospital management, as well as a training center for allied health technicians. Each village also has a conference center, a business hotel and shopping facilities.

Taking inspiration from the organic form of an acanthus leaf, the design solution features interconnected village walkways that thread together multiple buildings. An organically shaped canopy composed of ETFE (ethylene tetrafluoroethylene) and other translucent materials covers the entire complex, allowing daylight to permeate the space while shielding the facilities from excessive heat. Photovoltaic panels harvest solar energy for ventilation and lighting.

The inspiration of the acanthus leaf extends to the curvilinear street pattern that provides patients and students with a welcoming, campus-like ambience.

All automobile traffic is directed to the lower garden level of the village, with the main

concourse level and upper floors reserved for pedestrians. Separating automobiles from pedestrians creates an ideal environment for serendipitous encounters that facilitate the exchange of knowledge in medicine and science.

Situated near major transportation routes, each medical village will receive patients from 22 feeder hospitals located throughout Saudi Arabia.

◀ aerial view

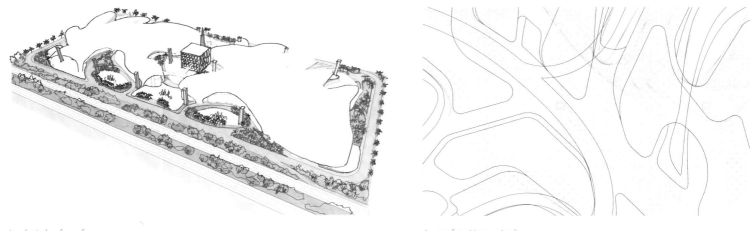

▲ sketch of roof

▲ roof pattern study

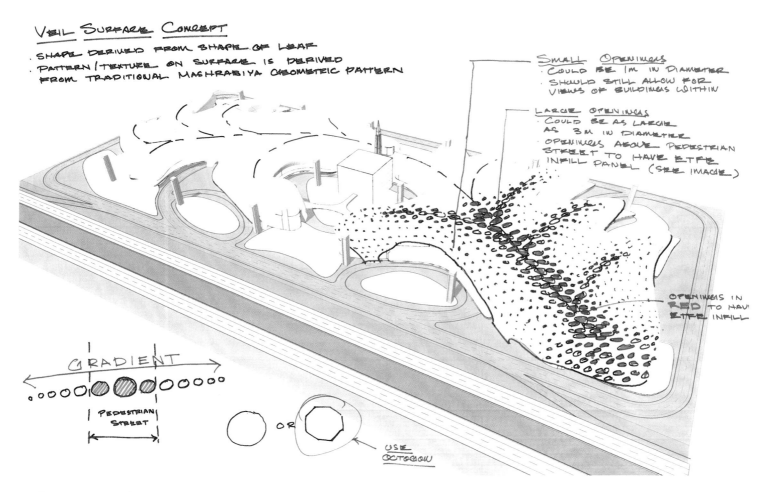

VEIL SURFACE CONCEPT

· SHAPE DERIVED FROM SHAPE OF LEAF
· PATTERN / TEXTURE ON SURFACE IS DERIVED
  FROM TRADITIONAL MASHRABIYA GEOMETRIC PATTERN

SMALL OPENINGS
· COULD BE 1M IN DIAMETER
· SHOULD STILL ALLOW FOR
  VIEWS OF BUILDINGS WITHIN

LARGE OPENINGS
· COULD BE AS LARGE
  AS 3M IN DIAMETER
· OPENINGS ABOVE PEDESTRIAN
  STREET TO HAVE ETFE
  INFILL PANEL (SEE IMAGE)

OPENINGS IN
RED TO HAVE
ETFE INFILL

GRADIENT

PEDESTRIAN
STREET

OR

USE
OCTAGON

▲ roof pattern organization

▲ interior street

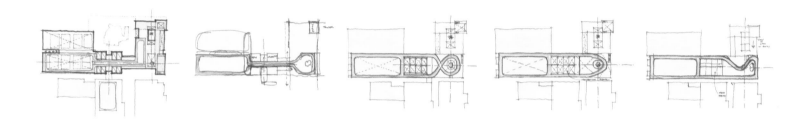

Auburn University Recreation and Wellness Center
Auburn, Alabama, USA

240,000 sq. ft. / 22,300 sq. m.

Completion: 2013

The Recreation and Wellness Center honors the distinct architectural character of Auburn's campus while creating a hub for personal, social and physical well-being.

Built for an economical $225.00 per square foot, the highly efficient space provides an engaging experience for all and great value for the university.

During the design process, students and administrators consistently expressed a desire for spaces that "felt like Auburn." The design responds by breaking the larger volume of space into fitness neighborhoods that recreate the feeling of the campus' many interconnected quads.

Marking the building's entry, the five-story cardio tower complements the campus' historic context of towers and steeples while providing interior spaces for suspension training, group cycling and yoga. Located on the tower's top floor, the yoga studio has hangar windows that fold up at the press of a button, allowing for the studio to be completely open to outdoor air.

At one-third of a mile, the indoor running track is one of the longest in the country and the first to be designed in a "corkscrew" configuration. The track winds through both gymnasiums, across the atrium and around the two-story atrium's climbing tower while offering users different route choices. To

achieve the crossover, the track ramps up and down, enabling runners to do interval training.

The facility also offers basketball courts, an outdoor leisure pool, cardio/fitness zones, a rock climbing wall, weight training areas and outdoor recreation spaces.

HOK provided preliminary planning and programming services to support a student referendum that funded the project. The team produced documentation, a revised program and 3D renderings to develop a promotional package for marketing and a pricing package that helped the university understand the fee assessment required for the project.

◄ lobby

▲ 1/3-mile elevated running track

▲ gymnasium

▲ track corkscrew configuration around climbing tower

TRACK ETIQUETTE

WALK ON THE RIGHT
RUN ON THE LEFT

BE AWARE OF
FELLOW RUNNERS

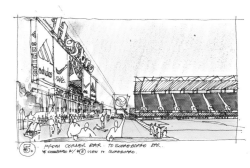

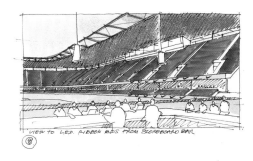

Avaya Stadium | MLS Earthquakes

San Jose, California, USA

274,500 sq. ft. / 25,500 sq. m.

18,000 seats

Completion: 2015

The design of the San Jose Earthquakes' Major League Soccer stadium emphasizes the fan experience by creating an intimate atmosphere that brings spectators close to the action.

Just two miles from downtown San Jose, the 18,000-seat, European-style Avaya Stadium features covered seating that holds in the sound and creates an energetic atmosphere for fans. This soccer-specific stadium offers exceptional sightlines from every angle.

Premium seating options include club, patio and luxury suites. The Premier Midfield and Premier Midline seating sections boast 3,200 upgraded, plush seats. Club seating offers food and beverage delivery service and

provides an authentic community experience just feet from the pitch. Patio suites feature 680 square feet of space, with comfortable couch-style seating and private wait staff. Field-level luxury suites offer high-end furnishings and are customizable with sliding glass doors and an open floor plan.

The 600-person Supporter's Section adjacent to a "Beers of the World" concession space has an open terrace standing area that offers a rallying point for die-hard fans. A two-acre 7UP Epicenter Fan Zone features a double-sided video display. Neighboring the fan zone is North America's largest outdoor bar. At 3,650 square feet, the full-service bar offers field-level views.

Avaya Stadium is the first cloud-enabled professional sports venue, a fitting accomplishment for the stadium of Silicon Valley's soccer club. The high-tech fan experience begins with a stadium app that helps create an innovative experience for fans.

Designed to achieve the client's goals for sustainability, the stadium features 882 solar panels — enough to offset power use at regular-season games.

◄ view from corner deck

▲ scoreboard bar

▲ seating bowl

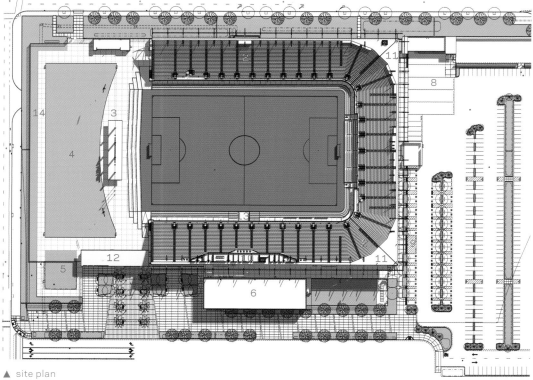

▲ site plan

1 main entrance
2 seating bowl
3 scoreboard bar
4 epicenter fan zone
5 vip lawn
6 team building
7 training yard

8 broadcast truck parking
9 vip entrance
10 pressbox
11 party deck
12 team store
13 player ramp
14 food truck parking

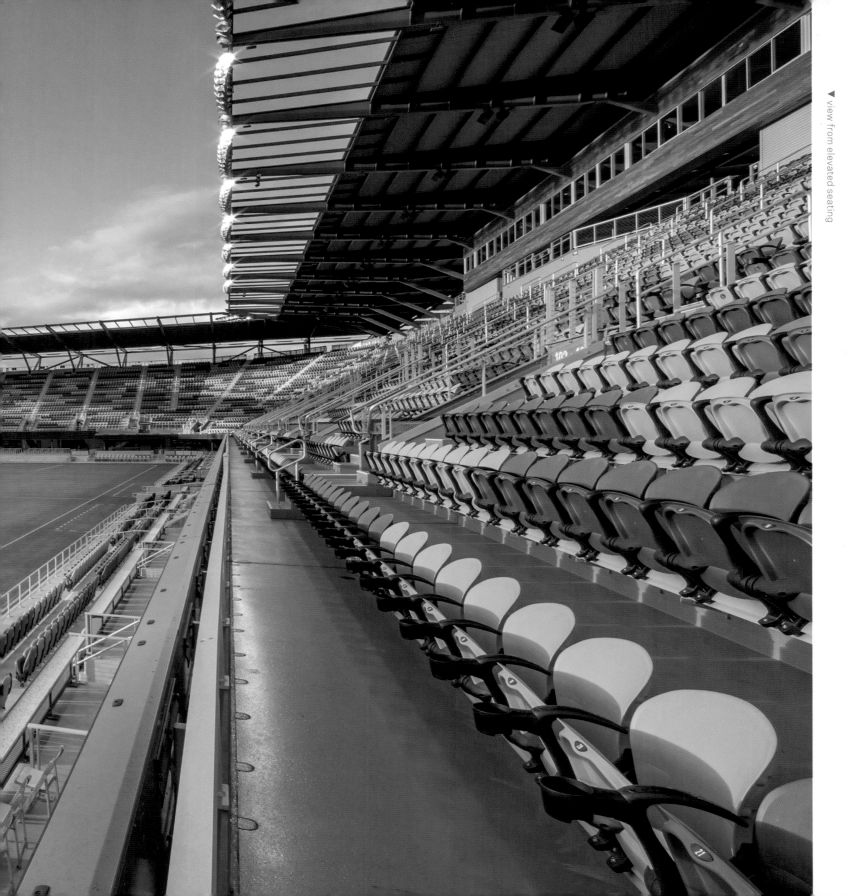

AVAYA STADIUM | MLS EARTHQUAKES

Avery Dennison Global Headquarters

Glendale, California, USA

44,100 sq. ft. / 4,100 sq. m.

Completion: 2014

The design of Avery Dennison's new headquarters transforms the 80-year-old global labeling and packaging company's workplace into a more space-efficient, collaborative and flexible environment.

Located on two floors of a new office building, the open workplace features low-height, team-oriented workstations on the perimeter with ample access to natural light and views. Solid walled conference rooms, glass-enclosed huddle rooms and informal lounge spaces facilitate different types of collaboration and varying degrees of privacy. A "collaboration axis" adjacent to the elevator lobby on each floor links both sides of the office core.

The office features Rise, Scooch and Belong from the Allsteel Gather collaborative furniture collection, designed by HOK Product Design and IDa Design.

The centrally located stairs provide an active space that serves as a meeting and dining area while supporting presentations and interoffice telecommunication through a state-of-the-art audiovisual system.

Unique branding elements and company relics enhance the office. A backlit, digitized portrait of Avery Dennison's founder, R. Stanton Avery, greets visitors in the elevator lobby. The company's patented radio frequency identification (RFID) tape is transformed into a decorative pattern in glass and millwork paneling. An illustrated acrylic reproduction of the beloved koi pond from the company's former headquarters serves as the safety barrier under the central stairs.

The open, egalitarian workplace promotes faster, better decision-making and creates a sense of community that connects employees across every level and department.

The design team oversaw significant structural modifications to the existing office building and the delivery of several highly customized details during the fast-track construction process.

◀ central stair

▲ conference room

▲ small meeting rooms

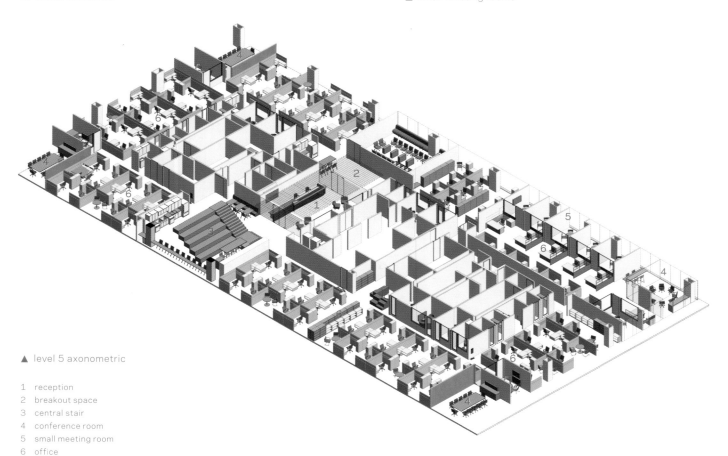

▲ level 5 axonometric

1 reception
2 breakout space
3 central stair
4 conference room
5 small meeting room
6 office

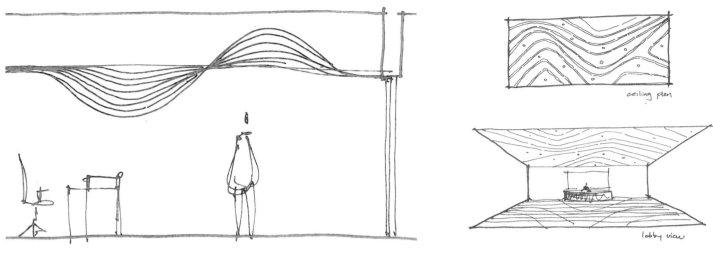

▲ sketch, plan + perspective of hunter douglas curved high profile baffle by hok product design

▲ ceiling above central stair

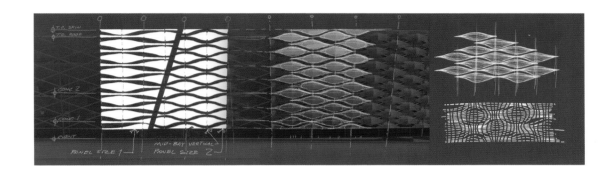

Basrah Sports City
Basrah, Iraq

2.77 million sq. ft. / 257,340 sq. m.

Main stadium: 65,000 seats
Secondary stadium: 10,000 seats

Completion: 2013

Basrah Sports City is the largest sports facility in Iraq and features one of the country's largest stadiums.

The complex includes a 65,000-seat soccer stadium surrounded by a manmade lake in the shape of Iraq. The site also features a 10,000-seat secondary stadium, four training soccer fields, team housing facilities, a VIP guesthouse and associated infrastructure buildings.

The selection of Iraq to host the 2013 Gulf Cup of Nations, a biennial soccer tournament for Arab countries, drove the development of the project, which is located outside the southern port city of Basrah. Iraq's Ministry of Youth and Sport wanted this project to spur growth and development in the area while introducing Iraqi athletes to the world stage.

The design of the marquee venue reflects local architectural influences, recalling a proud past while serving as a bridge to a modern era. Inspiration for the main stadium design came from Basrah's timeless and essential icons, from the date palm tree to traditional woven goods. Paying homage to the patterned facades of traditional Iraqi homes, the textured skin also provides a functional response to the local climate.

More than 480,000 square feet of synthetic cladding encases the stadium, forming large panels that interweave with steel columns. The external wrap and roof sheets are supported by a massive steel structure weighing 19,000 tons.

By integrating graceful yet strong forms and surfaces, the architecture expresses the speed, power and perpetual movement of soccer.

The main contractor was Iraqi company Abdullah Al-Jiburi. HOK teamed with this contractor and associate architect/engineer RMC-Partners to deliver the project under a design-build contract. Use of 3D modeling, animation and web meeting technologies helped the multinational team work efficiently while overcoming geographic and language barriers. Additional engineering and design consultants included Thornton Tomasetti, WSP Group, Langan Engineering, Lloyd Engineering, WJHW and Cini-Little.

◄ south elevation

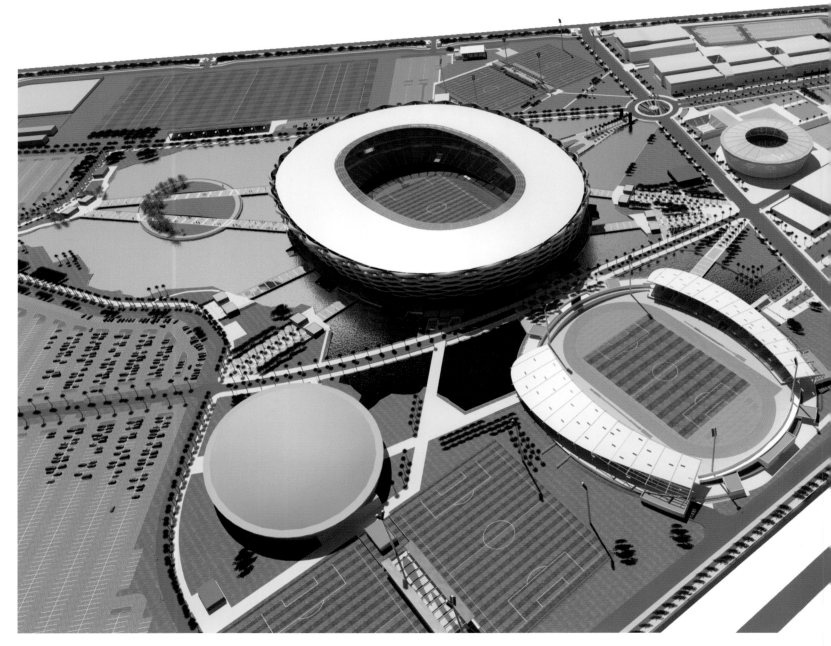

▲ site axonometric

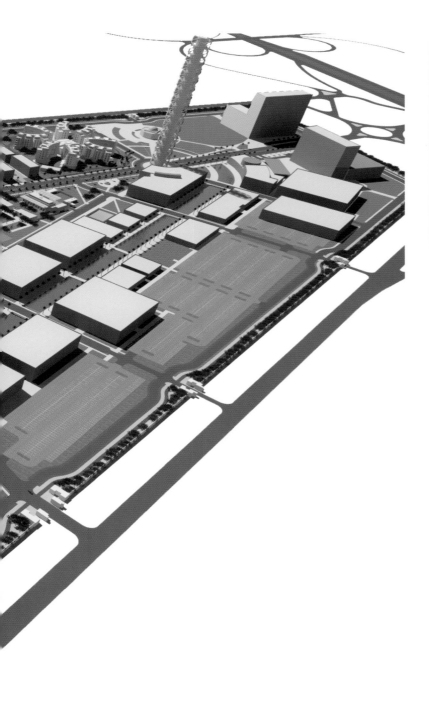

▲ stadium interior

▲ stadium interior at night

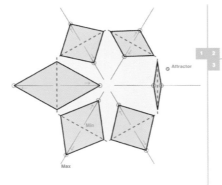
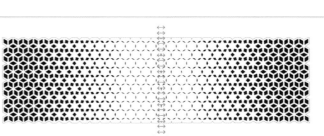

▲ gradated mashrabiya coding study

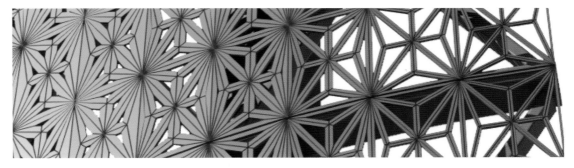

▲ schematic mashrabiya study

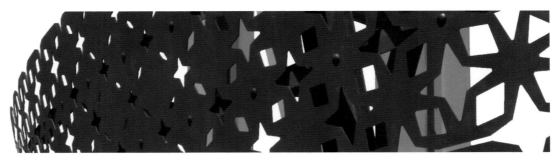

▲ physical mock-up of mashrabiya

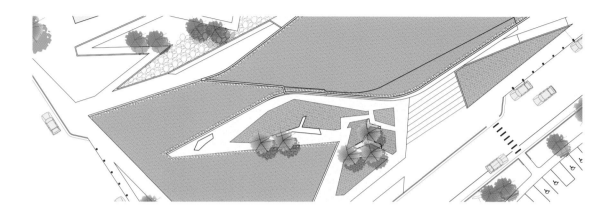

Black & Veatch World Headquarters
Overland Park, Kansas, USA

HOK
2015 design annual

631,380 sq. ft. / 58,660 sq. m.

Completion: 2014

The addition of the Rodman Innovation Pavilion completes a five-year, phased renovation and expansion to Black & Veatch's headquarters in a Kansas City suburb.

The expanded headquarters communicates Black & Veatch's commitment to engineering innovation and environmental responsibility. The design creates a vibrant culture for the 2,400 people who work on the campus.

In addition to renovating Black & Veatch's 617,660-sq.-ft. office building, the team designed a prominent pavilion that serves as the new entry.

Named for the company's former CEO, the Rodman Innovation Pavilion includes a client briefing center with integrated video/teleconferencing, conference space, a café and an atrium for company and community events.

As a showcase for Black & Veatch's engineering expertise, the pavilion features innovative sustainable design strategies including geothermal wells and an electricity microgrid that uses a natural gas microturbine and solar panels. A 14,900-sq.-ft. green roof, native landscaping, bioswales and rain gardens work together to reduce stormwater runoff.

By relocating conference rooms to surrounding spaces and creating an open stairwell that connects all eight floors, the headquarters renovation provides a new central hub for meetings. A fitness center, refurbished auditorium, updated workstations and new building systems enhance the work environment.

Close collaboration between HOK and general contractor JE Dunn Construction helped the team deliver the project on time and under budget.

◀ lobby

▲ pavilion meeting + collaboration space

▲ outdoor terrace + pavilion

▲ main entrance + pavilion lobby

 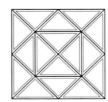 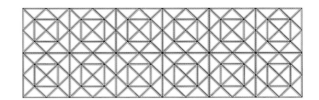

Chancery of the Permanent Mission of Singapore to the United Nations
New York, New York, USA

35,600 sq. ft. / 3,300 sq. m.

Completion: 2014

Home to Singapore's diplomatic mission to the United Nations, the new chancery for the government of Singapore is a secure embassy building that conveys a sense of openness and transparency.

The design weaves together the national ideals of Singapore with a reinterpretation of the country's vernacular architecture, integrating light, texture and shadow to illuminate the solid volumes of New York. Five vertical elements on the southern facade represent five ideals of the rising nation: democracy, peace, progress, justice and equality.

Reflecting the dualistic nature of an embassy structure, the design establishes a welcoming identity within New York City while addressing the inherent security issues related to the building's location within the tight confines of Manhattan.

Organized as a series of buffer zones between the street and the building's interior, the architectural expression features glass detailing that seamlessly complements the design intent.

The transparency of the street-facing elevation bends in a fluid form to reflect a diminishing zone of protection by section.

A translucent frit pattern applied to the glass supports privacy at the building's lower levels and becomes progressively less dense as it climbs the facade. Providing a visual reference to the culture of Singapore, this detailing is an abstraction of traditional wooden lattice screen elements integral to the country's architectural heritage.

◄ front entrance

▲ city location plan

▲ site plan

▲ facade conception

▲ street view

CHANCERY OF THE PERMANENT MISSION OF SINGAPORE TO THE U.N.

▲ facade screen patterns

▼ meeting room

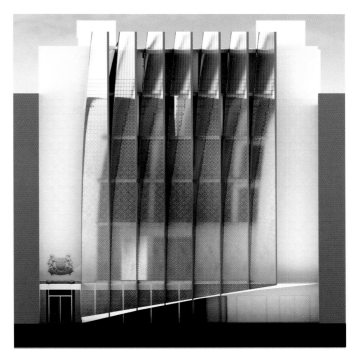

▲ front facade sketch

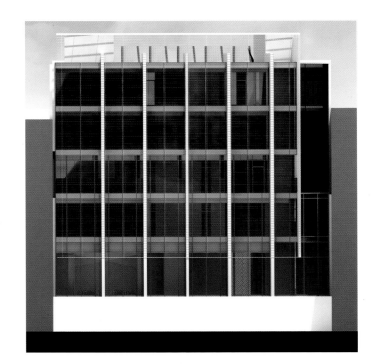

▲ back facade sketch

CHANCERY OF THE PERMANENT MISSION OF SINGAPORE TO THE U.N.

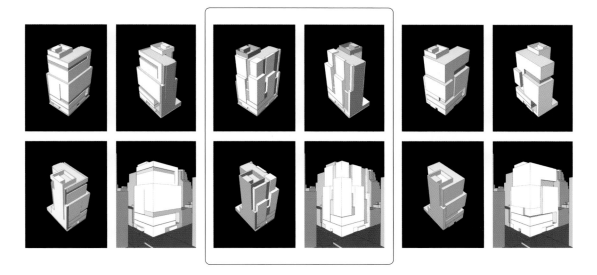

147-151 East 86th Street
New York, New York, USA

230,000 sq. ft. / 21,370 sq. m.

Completion: 2018

This 18-story luxury residential tower serves a transitional neighborhood in Upper Manhattan while adding commercial retail space in one of the city's busiest corridors.

The project supports the migration of higher-end development from the established Upper East Side avenues to the emerging Yorkville neighborhood closer to the East River.

The massing and design of the facade epitomize the neighborhood's transitional character. Featuring large expanses of glass, the dimensional form steps up toward the intersection and provides terraces for many of the residences. The French limestone cladding recalls the traditional stone buildings of the Upper East Side, while the large glazed openings take advantage of a modern cast-in-place concrete structure. The windows celebrate the individuality of units, which are conceived as jewel boxes set off from the

limestone through the use of deep bronze finished reveals.

Double-height storefront bays articulate retail areas at the building's base. The residential lobby entrance is located to the north on Lexington Avenue, away from the bustling activity of 86th Street.

The building houses 170,000 square feet of market-rate residential condominiums, 25,000 square feet for a flagship New York Sports Club facility and 30,000 square feet of commercial retail space.

Ranging in size from 1,600 to 4,400 square feet, the 51 individual residences feature 10-foot ceilings, large living and bedrooms, en-suite bathrooms, solid hardwood floors, custom kitchens with premium appliances, ample closet space and silent HVAC systems.

The building's amenity spaces include a private lounge, exhibition kitchen, game room, fitness center, children's playroom and lushly landscaped rooftop terrace.

Situated directly above the 86th Street subway station, the building provides convenient access to mass transportation with indoor and outdoor stair entrances and a new accessible elevator entrance.

◄ view from southwest

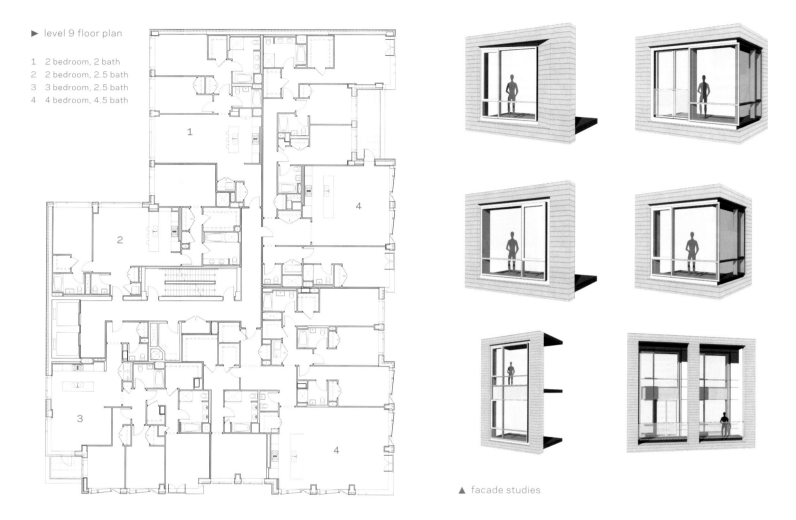

► level 9 floor plan

1 2 bedroom, 2 bath
2 2 bedroom, 2.5 bath
3 3 bedroom, 2.5 bath
4 4 bedroom, 4.5 bath

▲ facade studies

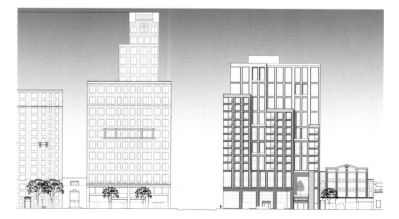

▲ south elevation

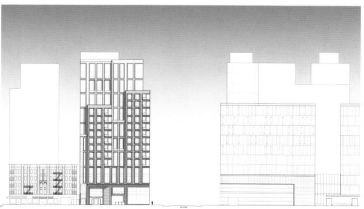

▲ west elevation

0
5
10
20
50ft

71

147-151 EAST 86TH STREET

Fitzrovia Apartments, Phase 2
London, UK

129,200 sq. ft. / 12,000 sq. m.

Completion: 2014

This project completes the redevelopment of the former Royal National Orthopaedic Hospital site in central London into a mixed-use, high-density urban development.

The project celebrates the rich variety of city living by integrating a healthcare facility, market-rate and affordable housing, contemporary offices, a historic building, parking and landscaped gardens on a compact urban site.

Phase 2 of the development includes the completion of the 100-unit residential building (market-rate and affordable apartments), as well as 3,230 square feet of office space within an existing Grade II-listed historic hall. These additions complement the project's first phase, which was also designed by HOK and included an outpatient orthopaedic clinic and 45 apartment units in the residential building.

Located near Regent's Park in one of London's most sensitive urban environments, the residential building is arranged around two landscaped courtyards. It incorporates sustainable features such as ground-source heat pumps, biofuel boilers, and green walls and roofs. Primary facades are composed of Spanish limestone that integrates public art in the form of colored glass fins depicting abstract images of MRI scans.

Vertical bay windows fabricated from anodized aluminum and glass accent the building design. To reflect the sun and maximize light, the elevations overlooking the courtyard are clad in light zinc tiles.

At the center of the site, the hospital's former waiting hall is connected to the building's main entrance on Bolsover Street. The technical requirements of retaining this 1927-listed

building in situ involved careful preservation of the historic structure's Roman Classical architectural character while creating a flexible interior office design.

Large murals that dominate the double-height space inspired the muted design palette. Textured upholstery, timber detailing and bespoke furniture ensure that the space fulfills tenant needs and complements the design aesthetic of the original building.

A glazed reception area with double-height ceilings opens onto a courtyard with stunning landscaped gardens, providing a place to escape the busy London streets.

◀ street view of phases 1 + 2

▲ site plan

▶ ground level plan

1 phase 1: rnoh clinic
2 central courtyard
3 retained listed hall + offices
4 affordable housing entrance
5 private apartments' entrance
6 ramp to basement parking
7 affordable housing units
8 bicycle parking + play area
9 private apartments

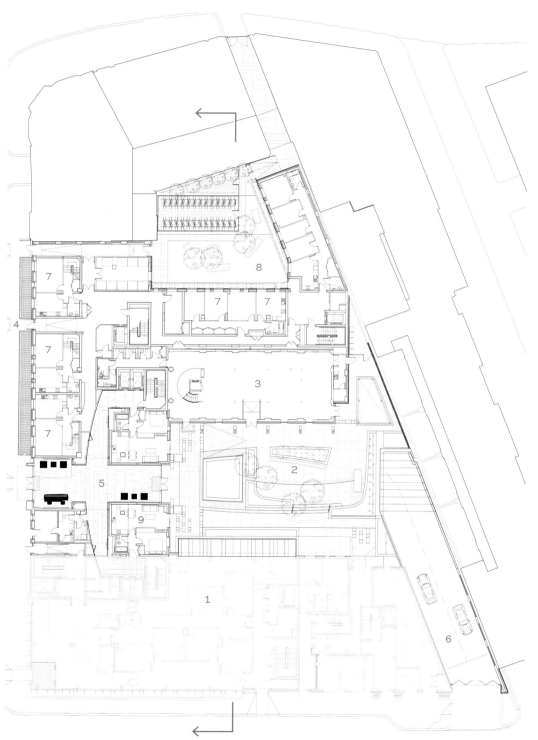

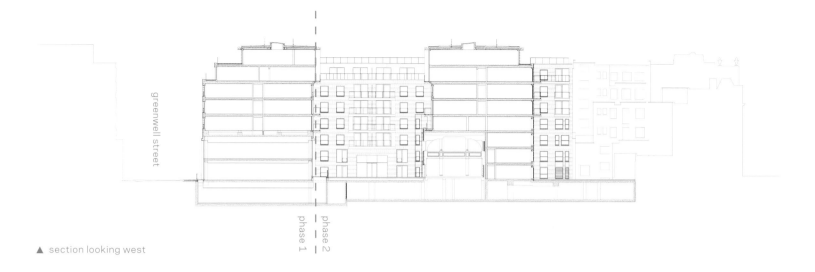

▲ section looking west

greenwell street

phase 2
phase 1

▲ courtyard incorporating historic hall + new structure

▲ mezzanine conference room within existing hall

▲ conference room

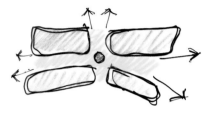 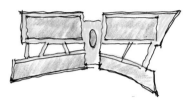 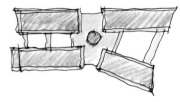 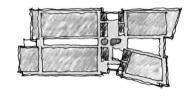

The Francis Crick Institute
London, UK

980,000 sq. ft. / 91,000 sq. m.

Completion: 2016

Six leading medical research and educational organizations have partnered to form the Francis Crick Institute, one of Europe's largest biomedical and translational research centers.

Named after Francis Crick, the scientist who helped discover the structure of DNA, the institute is a landmark partnership between the UK's three largest funders of biomedical research — the Medical Research Council, Cancer Research UK and the Wellcome Trust — and three of its leading universities: University College London, Imperial College London and King's College London.

Located in central London, the steel, glass and terra-cotta clad building occupies a full city block and creates strong architectural links to historic local buildings. Large cantilevered bay windows and tall glass atria reduce the building's impact at street level and maintain natural light in workspaces and public areas.

To reduce its visible mass, one-third of the structure is below ground, while the curved roof presents a gentle face to the community.

The design encourages collaboration and interaction among multidisciplinary researchers including biologists, chemists, physicists, engineers, computer scientists and mathematicians.

The facility is divided into four "laboratory neighborhoods" connected by two atria. The atria cross at the center of the building to create a hub with break areas, informal collaboration space, a large central stair and a concierge serving the entire floor. Walkways and informal meeting areas crisscross the main atrium and connect neighborhoods.

The atria bring daylight into all of the labs and other spaces while enhancing the visibility of people throughout the building

and between floors. Glass walls allow for views into labs, promoting transparency and openness. Unless specific functions require closed walls, lab neighborhoods are open to encourage interaction.

Designed with flexibility, lab neighborhoods can support rapid reconfiguration as research programs change. A centralized service distribution system enables a kit-of-parts approach in which predetermined components can be plugged into service spines in different combinations.

HOK collaborated on the final exterior design and massing with PLP Architecture. The building is expected to achieve a BREEAM Excellent rating.

◄ main entrance

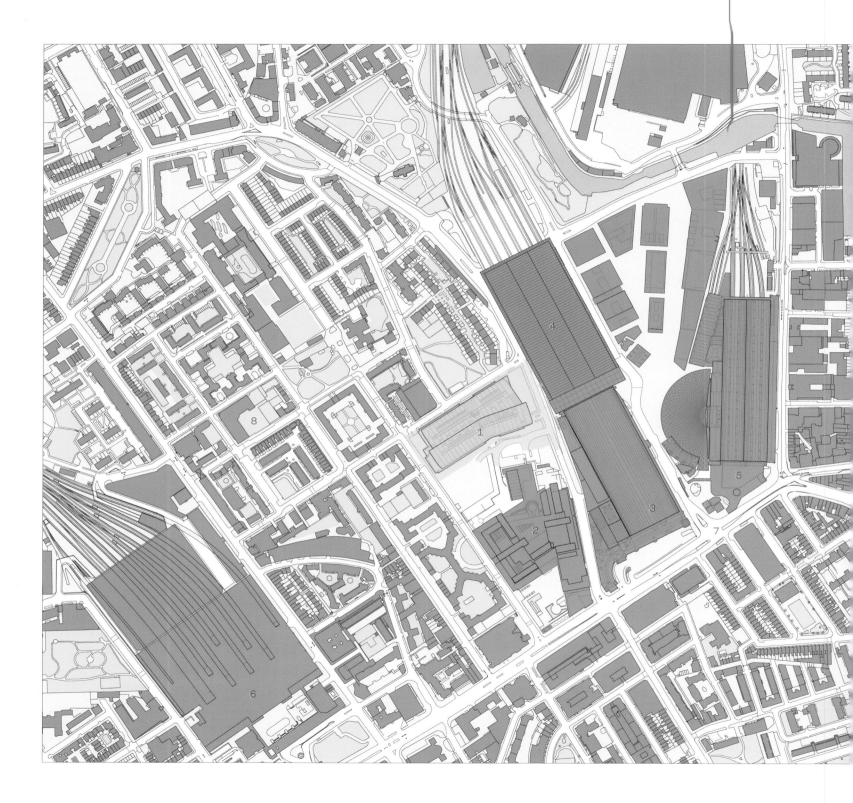

◀ regional site plan

1 the francis crick institute
2 british library
3 st. pancras station
4 euro star station
5 kings cross station
6 euston station
7 euston road
8 camden neighborhood

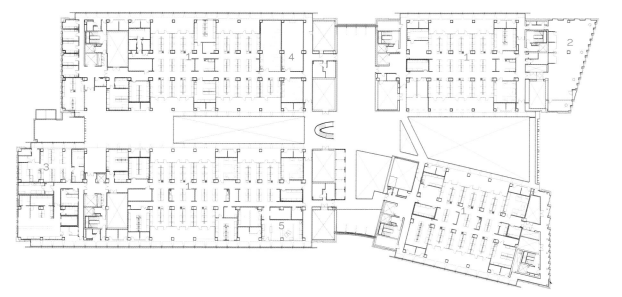

◄ level 2 plan

1 wet lab
2 dry lab
3 histopathology
4 flow cytometry
5 high throughput screening

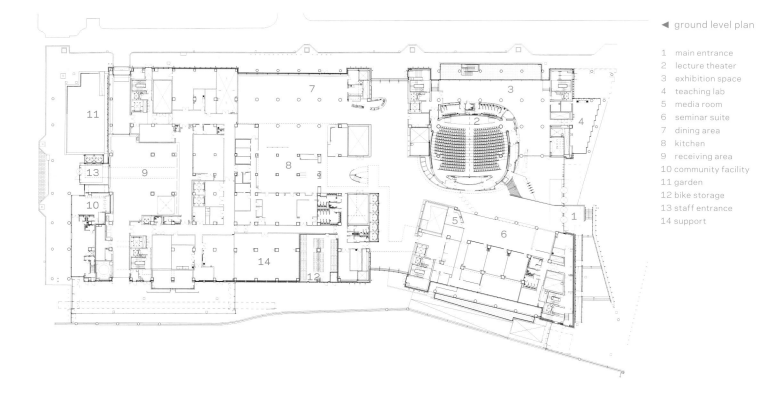

◄ ground level plan

1 main entrance
2 lecture theater
3 exhibition space
4 teaching lab
5 media room
6 seminar suite
7 dining area
8 kitchen
9 receiving area
10 community facility
11 garden
12 bike storage
13 staff entrance
14 support

▲ north elevation looking toward st. pancras station

▲ north elevation looking west

▲ staff entrance

▲ interior atrium

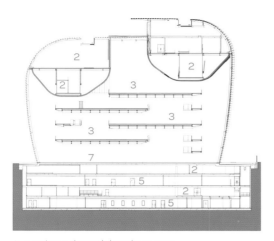

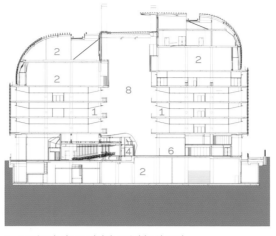

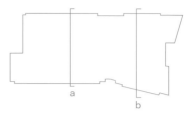

▲ section a through breakout area   ▲ section b through lab neighborhood

1   laboratory
2   mechanical
3   breakout + informal meeting area
4   auditorium
5   support lab
6   conference suite
7   dining area
8   atrium

▲ lab furniture mock-up

▲ collaboration space

▲ dining area

Hamad International Airport Passenger Terminal Complex
Doha, Qatar

6.5 million sq. ft. / 604,000 sq. m.

Completion: 2015

The design of the passenger terminal complex at Qatar's replacement airport celebrates form, surface and light while providing an efficient yet inspirational experience for travelers. As the landmark home for Qatar Airways, the country's national airline, the terminal can accommodate 30 million passengers annually and has 41 unrestricted contact gates.

Through expressive architecture rooted in place, the iconic terminal creates a lasting impression on guests. While contemporary in design to mirror Qatar's progressive growth, the airport pays homage to the nation's rich cultural heritage and natural environment. The dramatic, curving building silhouette recalls ocean waves and sand dunes to project a powerful image as Qatar's gateway to the world.

Departing passengers experience an undulating super roof in the light-filled departure hall. The steel-framed glass wall provides unobstructed views from the curbside arrival area through the ticketing hall, enabling passengers to easily find their destinations. The longer east and west

facades have similar high-performance glass that controls solar heat gain and glare.

Moving through an open immigration area, originating passengers join transfer passengers on the first floor under a vast central skylight that provides visual access to one of five concourses. The two large transfer hubs are linked by an automated people mover.

Arriving passengers progress to the ground-floor baggage hall and exit to a triple-volume meeters and greeters hall with direct access to taxi pavilions and an intermodal transportation hub.

A vast wood ceiling in the longest concourse provides visual warmth that contrasts with the sleek metal and glass surfaces. In other concourses, vaulted metal ceilings mimic the undulating roof line. Glass envelops the spacious hold rooms, quiet rooms, passenger activity nodes and 20 airline lounges. Skylights and interconnecting glass ceiling "zippers" provide natural light and dramatic evening desert views.

A deliberate lack of ornamentation provides passengers with an intrinsic understanding of movement and spatial function within the terminal. The team selected materials for their longevity, sustainability and local significance. Graceful structural arches are left unadorned, and the vast floor surface is a combination of terrazzo in high-circulation areas and carpet in ancillary spaces.

South of the passenger terminal, a public mosque serves as the symbolic heart of the airport. Its domed prayer hall and slender minaret are visible from the entrance road. The structures are set within a stone-paved plaza dotted with fountain jets representing the purifying role of water.

Guest amenities include two hotels, ample duty-free shopping, and a spa and health club. An extensive public art program features local and international artists' work throughout the terminal.

◀ main terminal

◀ site plan

1 runway
2 central lagoon
3 short-term parking
4 long-term parking

► departure level floor plan

1 meeters + greeters hall
2 concourse a
3 concourse b
4 concourse c
5 concourse d
6 concourse e

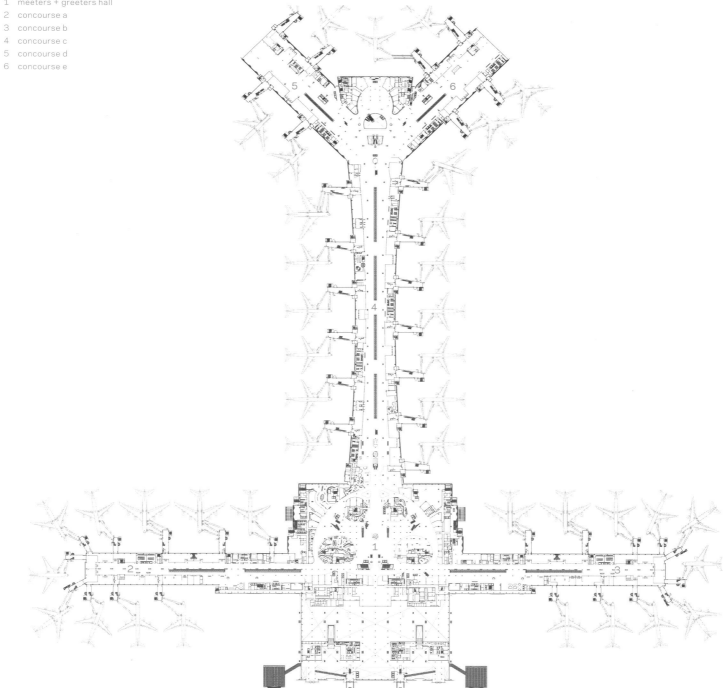

0 20

50

100

250m

91

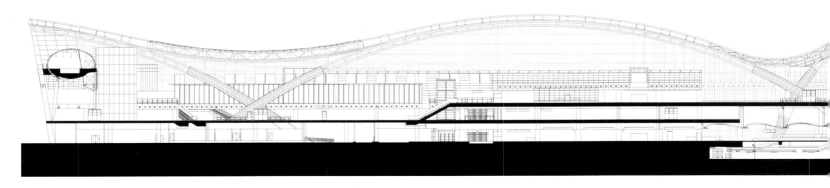

▲ north-south section

▲ retail + dining

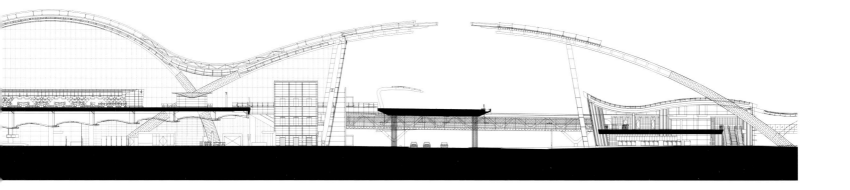

▲ concourse exterior

▲ concourse

▲ terminal atrium

▲ mosque

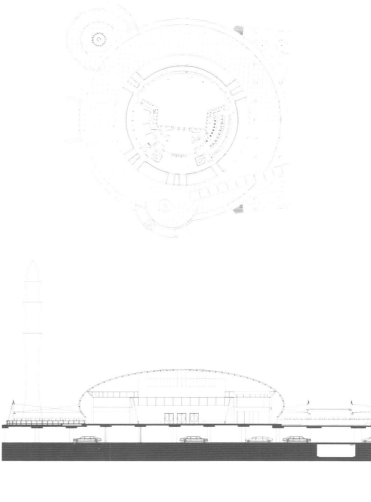

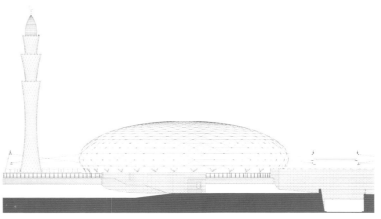

▲ mosque floor plan, section + east elevation

▲ mosque interior

0 5 10

20

40m

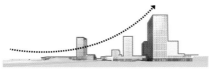  

Hana Dream Town
Incheon, South Korea

2.2 million sq. ft. / 205,000 sq. m.

Completion: 2018

This will be the new global headquarters for Hana Financial Group, one of Korea's largest private commercial banks and a leading international financial institution.

Located in the Cheongna District of the Incheon Free Economic Zone, the campus integrates the company's core strategic infrastructure, including a data center, financial R&D center, education and training center, IT center, integrated call center and business support facilities.

The design concept creates a unified campus with a strong visual presence reflecting Hana's values of openness, excellence, respect and integrity. Buildings are arranged to support a linear sequence of activities, with numerous outdoor spaces connecting the buildings to each other and to the landscape.

The flexible design of the headquarters tower uses a common structural grid that makes it easy to move individuals and departments. The optimum core-to-glass ratio maximizes natural light and views. Numerous breakout and informal meeting spaces encourage collaboration, while a series of atria provide alternative meeting and work environments.

The rolling hills of the adjacent golf course intersect with the campus, extending the landscape and forming open vistas. A large promenade crosses the site diagonally to create a visual and physical link from the headquarters tower to the surrounding recreation facilities. Informal pedestrian paths woven into the landscape connect building functions.

◀ aerial view

◄ site plan

1 service zone
2 headquarters zone
3 amenity zone
4 community garden
5 training zone
6 sports zone

◄ level 4 floor plan

1 eco atrium
2 community gathering
3 lounge
4 single + double rooms
5 4-person suites
6 vip lounge

0
10
20
40
60m

103

◄ level 1 floor plan

1 lobby
2 eco atrium
3 office
4 single + double rooms
5 4-person suites
6 lounge
7 dining room
8 vip lounge

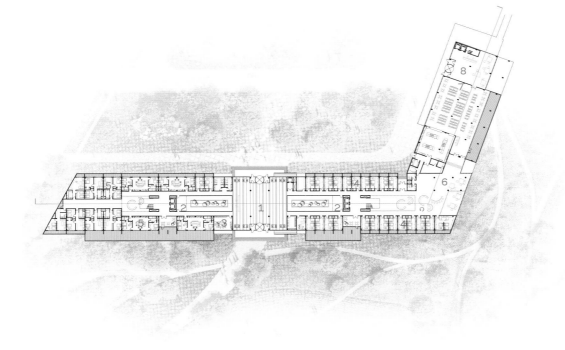

◄ east-west section

1 pv panels
2 green roof
3 eco atrium
4 group study
5 activity zone
6 lounge
7 bedrooms

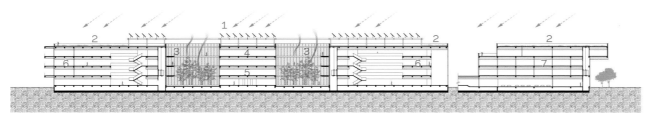

▲ site entrance courtyard

▲ corporate courtyard from swimming pool

▲ main boulevard

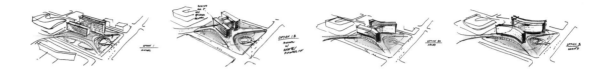

Hospital Design Competition in Shanghai, China, for a Confidential Client
Shanghai, China

893,000 sq. ft. / 83,000 sq. m.

Competition: 2014

The design of this private hospital, which will serve the healthcare needs of Shanghai's rapidly growing affluent population, accommodates complex healthcare delivery models and emerging technologies.

Inspired by the beauty and performance of nature, the design combines the efficiencies and rigor of biology with the soothing, restorative qualities of natural forms.

A solar analysis informed the site plan and shape of the buildings to optimize access to daylight and wind. The gentle curves of the massing reduce sharp corners and allow for the easy flow of space, air and light.

Textured natural materials and smooth finished surfaces form the exterior materials palette. The patient towers and central core are clad in glass and light-colored metal panels, while the building podium is enveloped by a hillside.

In the central public atrium, warm limestone flooring, glass panels and wood screens help create a peaceful, healing environment. All patient rooms and most staff spaces provide access to outside views, operable windows and landscaped terraces.

Guided by regenerative principles, the design achieves net positive energy and water targets through sustainable and biophilic strategies that also promote health and wellness.

Advanced lighting, daylighting, heating, cooling and ventilation strategies will reduce energy use by at least 50 percent compared to similar facilities. The hospital's remaining energy needs will be provided by a combination of building-integrated photovoltaic systems and on-site cogeneration via biomass or biogas.

Efficient water systems significantly reduce the building's overall water demand. Rainwater harvesting and on-site graywater and blackwater treatment generate water for use in cooling towers, power generation, laundry and irrigation. An on-site water treatment facility will enable the hospital to return at least as much water back to the municipal water system as it uses for its potable water demand.

◄ view from entry

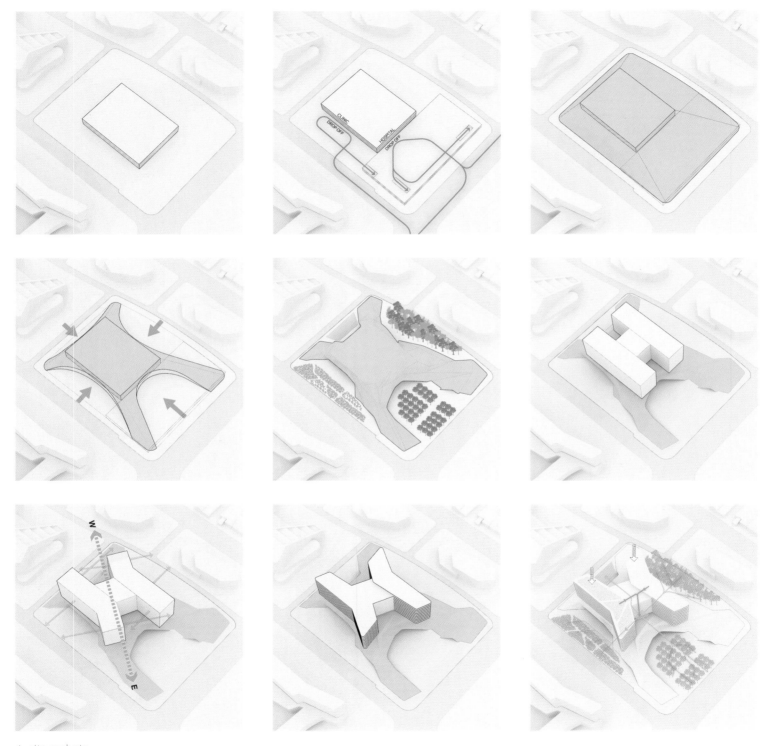

▲ site analysis

▲ aerial perspective

► site plan

1   orchard courtyard
2   garden courtyard
3   forest courtyard
4   sky garden
5   view garden

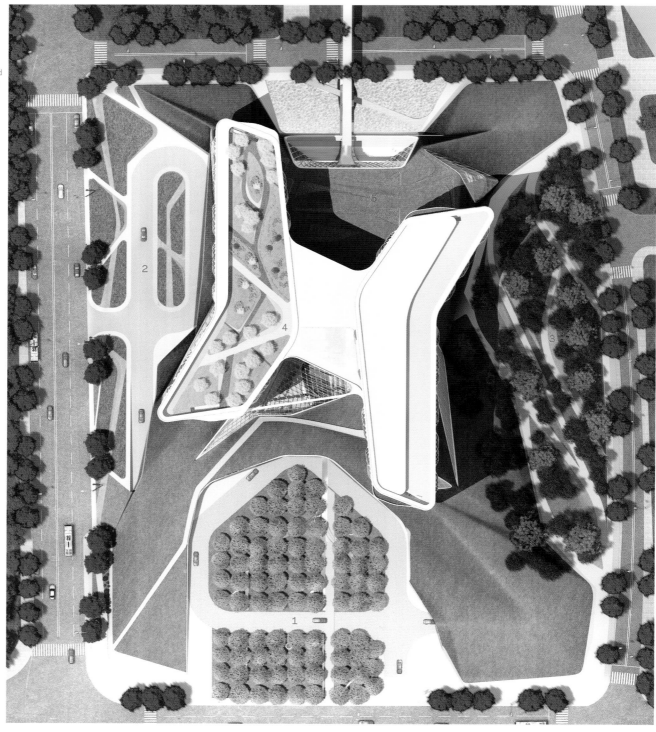

▼ typical system

city water — domestic water
150 — 100
— irrigation
— 45
— water feature
— 5

rain — sewer
50 — 150
waste
100

export: 0

▼ net positive system

city water — domestic water
90 — 90

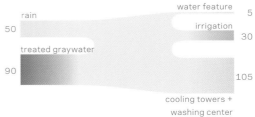

rain — water feature — 5
50 — irrigation
— 30
treated graywater
90 — 105

cooling towers +
washing center

◄ ground level plan

1 patient rooms
2 family area
3 waiting area
4 staff space
5 shared support space

HOSPITAL DESIGN COMPETITION IN SHANGHAI, CHINA

▲ central atrium

▲ patient room

▲ central atrium

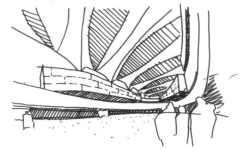

Huafa New Town, Phase 6
Zhuhai, Guangdong Province, China

3 million sq. ft. / 280,000 sq. m.
34 acres / 14 hectares

Completion: 2014

Annual EUI: 60 kBTU / sf / yr
8% below ASHRAE 2007

Situated along the Gongbei Customs Building at the juncture of the future Zhuhai-Hong Kong-Macau transportation interchange, this retail and luxury residential development is a vital part of the Huafa New Town International Lifestyle Community. The prestigious location gives the development a distinct public image.

A 645,000-sq.-ft. shopping mall, including a theater, supermarket and department store, anchors the development's west end, while the east end features a 270,000-sq.-ft. spa center. A 160,000-sq.-ft. promenade spans the area between, weaving together the anchor stores, greenery and waterfront.

The facade's different elevations feature an integrated composition of elements ranging from storefronts and feature walls to advertising boards and multimedia screens. With a palette of glass fiber-reinforced concrete, glazing and metallic detailing, the vibrant retail street maintains an intimate, human scale.

At the northwest edge of the development, two 30-story apartment towers feature prime orientations for spectacular garden views. Connections to the retail mall and other amenities provide residents with a distinctly urban and sophisticated experience.

The entire commercial complex is part of a looped sequence of retail spaces that share fluid massing silhouettes, ambiguous indoor-outdoor transitions and seamless circulation.

Fully integrated with the internal retail street, the outdoor greenery and waterfront provide visitors with scenic views and shelter from the elements. Linked by pedestrian bridges on the second story, the individual structures provide a variety of indoor and outdoor shopping experiences.

A 1,115-foot-long street canopy hovering 65 feet above the ground is clad with a lightweight ETFE (ethylene tetrafluoroethylene) membrane supported

by a steel structure. Deriving its fluid form from tree trunks and leaves, the canopy's web provides a sculptural focal point while shielding shoppers from the elements.

The design orients the development to take advantage of the region's prevailing winds and to maximize natural ventilation. A subtle lift at the mall's southern edge helps capture the summer breeze.

Zhuhai Huafa Architectural Design Consulting Co. served as the local partner for the project.

▲ aerial view from south

► roof plan

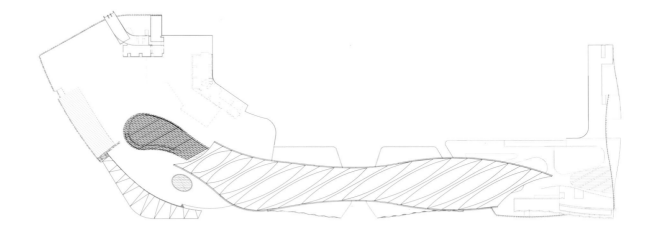

▼ site plan

1 shopping mall atrium
2 retail street
3 service apartment drop-off
4 spa hotel lobby
5 kindergarten
6 arrival plaza
7 sunken plaza
8 bus terminal

▲ retail street south entrance

▲ retail mall west entrance

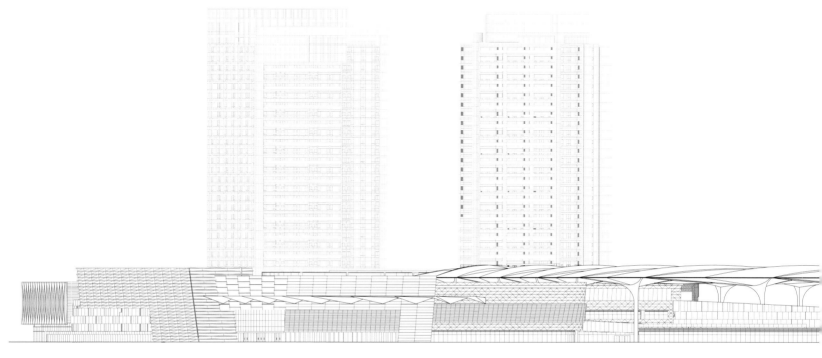

▲ south elevation

▲ retail mall southeast entrance

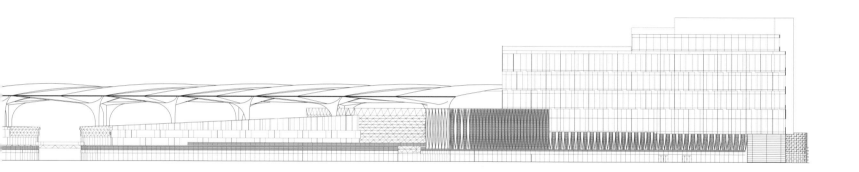

330 Hudson
New York, New York, USA

466,000 sq. ft. / 43,290 sq. m.

Completion: 2014

The restoration and expansion of 330 Hudson Street transforms the 1910 warehouse building into a dynamic office and retail destination with eight new floors of contemporary Class A headquarters office space.

Located in the Hudson Square area of Manhattan, the 16-story building borders the western edge of SoHo and is influenced by the neighborhood's turn-of-the-century industrial warehouses.

A complete restoration of the original eight-story building includes the two-story limestone colonnade, brick facade with punched openings, one-story limestone cornice and portions of the original Beaux-Arts storefronts. All decorative column capitals are restored or replicated. The heritage bronze metalwork featured on storefronts and the

entry canopy recalls the neighborhood's historic context.

The insertion of a transitional brick envelope merges the base building with the modern glass-and-aluminum curtain wall of the tower's eight-floor addition. Inside, 14-foot ceilings and floor-to-ceiling windows offer panoramic views of the river and city in every direction.

The team designed the new limestone lobby as a modern passageway and gallery space. LED media panels installed throughout the lobby stream high-impact digital imagery and graphics, providing a constantly changing arrival experience for tenants and visitors.

The U-shaped building wraps around a square courtyard developed as a private outdoor amenity space for tenants. Courtyard-facing

precast window panels bring natural light deep into the tower's large floor plates. The courtyard opens onto Old Jan's Alley, the historic site of John Seales' 1638 farm, one of the original plantations of the New Amsterdam colony.

Custom lighting punctuates an adjacent through-block passage wall to form a neutral backdrop. Buff pavers line the walkway, and decorative gates at each end of the passage integrate details reminiscent of the original building's storefront grilles.

The building design has achieved LEED Gold Core & Shell pre-certification.

◄ west facade

► levels 9-10 typical floor plan

1 conference room
2 office
3 supplies
4 kitchen
5 receiving area
6 it support

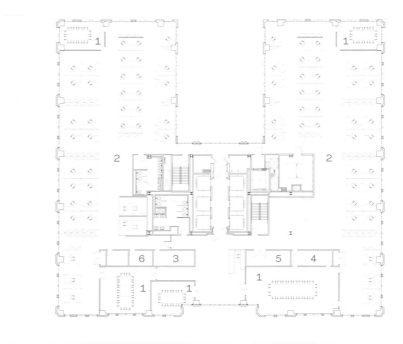

► levels 2-8 typical floor plan

1 reception
2 office
3 storage area
4 kitchen
5 receiving area
6 it support
7 pantry

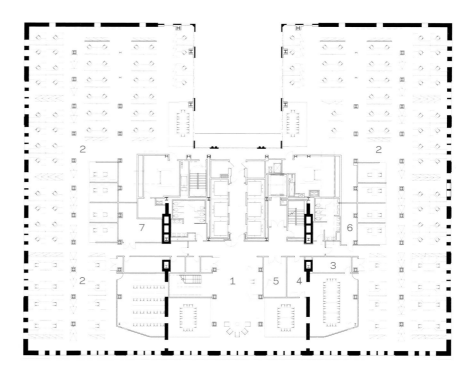

▲ view from northeast

▲ historic view from northwest

▲ view from west

▲ renovated podium

Kempegowda International Airport, Bengaluru Terminal 1 Expansion
Bengaluru, India

1.44 million sq. ft. / 134,000 sq. m.

Completion: 2013

The expansion of Terminal 1 repositions South India's busiest airport as an important hub for international travelers and cargo.

With a design that creates a pleasant and efficient curbside-to-aircraft passenger experience, the open, welcoming environment is easy to navigate and accommodates the increasing number of passengers using the airport.

The structure creates a grand, dramatic presence that seamlessly blends with the existing terminal. An elegantly curved roof serves as the unifying element for the new and existing facilities, creating a strong physical presence and visual identity for the airport. The roof's undulating shape forms a canopy that protects passengers and visitors from the elements. Its structural system includes a

monolithic plinth with elegant steel branches that pass through a suspended ceiling to meet the structure above.

Along with the building's large overhang, the use of low-e glazing reduces unwanted heat gain to create an energy-efficient, high-performance structure.

Skylights enable natural light to penetrate from above, linking the atmosphere and spacious feeling of the original building with the expansion. At the east and west ends of the terminal, 65-foot-high glass walls flood the space with natural light while creating commanding views of the outside.

Silver metallic and bright white finishes recall the high-tech nature of the city. Interior landscape features and plantings reinforce

Bengaluru's reputation as India's "Garden City." New passenger amenities include enhanced seating areas at gate lounges and a variety of new retail and dining opportunities.

Expanded, centralized departure areas include the addition of 30 check-in counters, six emigration counters and 11 security counters serving domestic and international passengers.

The expansion adds international gates designed specifically for newer wide-bodied aircraft such as the Airbus A380, as well as a more efficient baggage delivery system with dedicated island carousels.

◄ vehicular approach to terminal 1

▲ aerial from southwest

▲ arrivals, duty-free shops + upper-level interior ga

Living Building Challenge Collaborative Competition
Chicago, Illinois, USA

25,000 sq. ft. / 2,300 sq. m.

Competition: 2014

Annual EUI - Site: 16.7 kBTU / sf / yr
Annual EUI - Source: 32.8 kBTU / sf / yr

The winning design in a competition sponsored by the Living Building Challenge Collaborative: Chicago proposes an innovative sustainable classroom building as an annex to the overcrowded Eli Whitney Elementary School on the Southwest Side of Chicago.

The cross-disciplinary design solution elevates the building and connects it to the school with a surface that people can interact with and observe throughout the site.

An active, "living" exterior skin on the east and west facades acts as a shading device by changing shape based on the outside temperature. The aluminum and oxidized copper panels close when the exterior temperature rises, shading the facade. As the outside temperature cools, the panels open to increase the amount of light that can enter the building.

The landscape acts as a welcoming transition into the space and creates a flowing connection between the original school, existing annex and new building.

By elevating the new structure, the team preserves the existing site for students' outdoor play and community activities.

With a combination of innovative design and systems strategies to reach net zero energy, the building features sunshading devices, natural ventilation, radiant heating, insulation additions, displacement ventilation, a rooftop photovoltaic array and a geothermal exchange system.

To achieve a net zero balance of water consumption, the design uses low-flow plumbing fixtures and a custom rainwater harvesting and collection system that stores rainwater in cisterns while excess water drains into an overflow pond.

Health and safety are emphasized through the selection of sustainable building materials without VOCs or Red List ingredients. The team analyzed the life cycle of each product, choosing locally sourced materials with rapidly renewable and recycled content.

◀ building entrance + playground

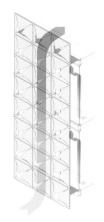 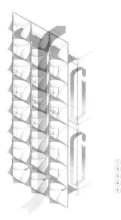 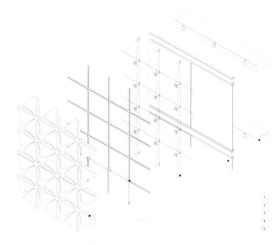

COOLING MODE   HEATING MODE

▲ facade opening   ▲ facade assembly

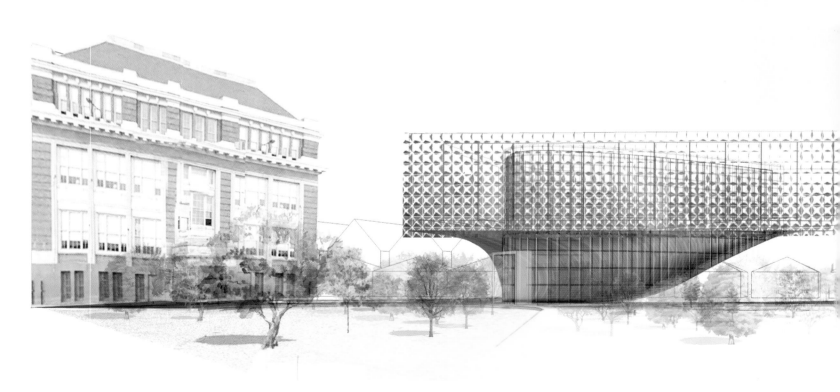

▲ west elevation

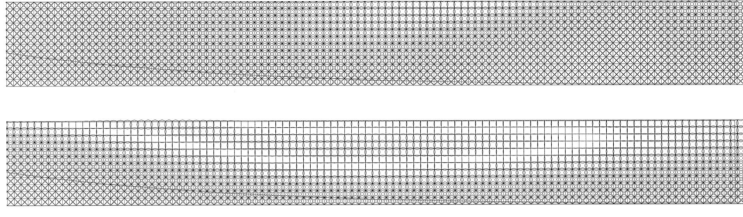

▲ facade conditions

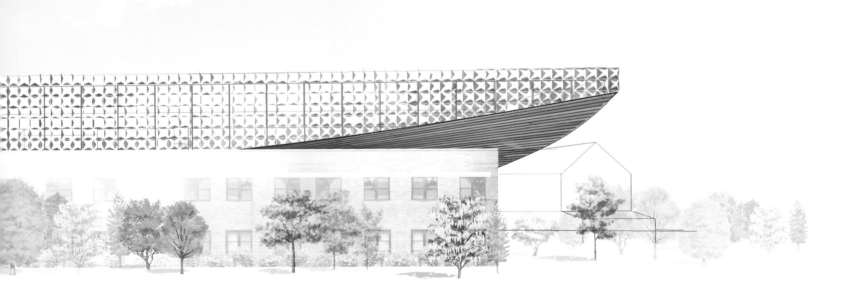

LIVING BUILDING CHALLENGE COLLABORATIVE COMPETITION

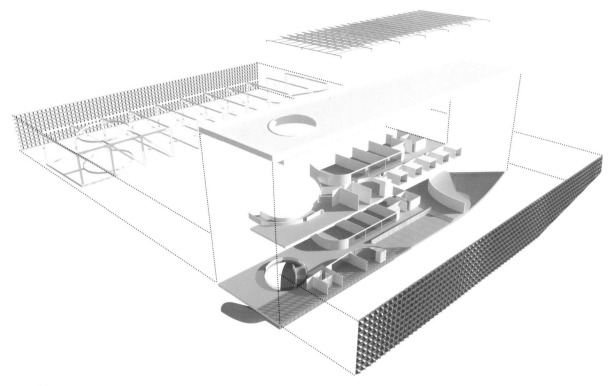

▲ building construction

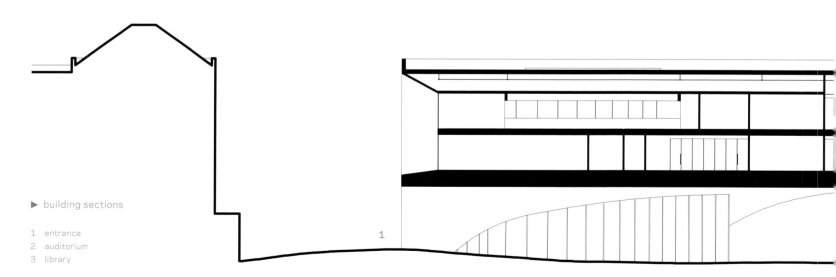

▶ building sections

1 entrance
2 auditorium
3 library

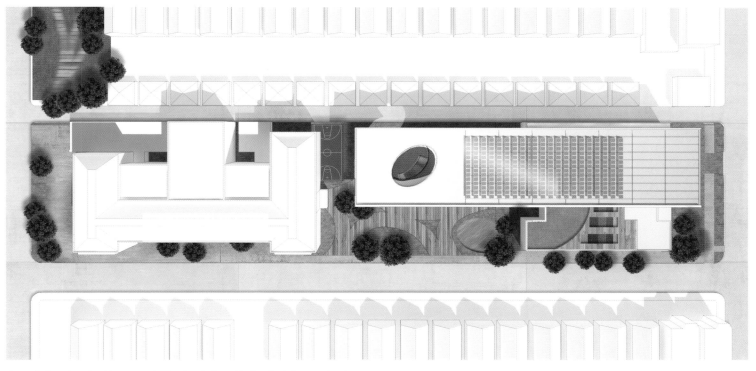

▲ roof plan showing the new addition's relationship to eli whitney school

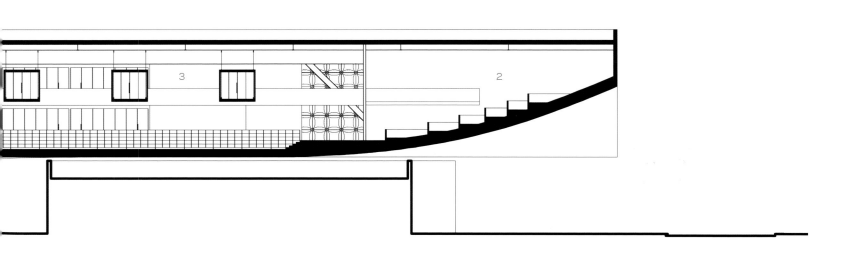

The Lodge at Walnut Creek
Walnut Creek, California, USA

164,000 sq. ft. / 15,235 sq. m.

Design completion: 2015

The Lodge at Walnut Creek is an eight-story modernist hotel and conference center located 30 miles east of San Francisco and adjacent to the Iron Horse Regional Trail, a popular destination for pedestrians, horseback riders and bicyclists.

Overlooking Mount Diablo, the lodge features 180 guestrooms, a premier restaurant and bar, a rooftop ballroom, a lounge and a terrace. The scenic location, mild climate and proximity to upscale shopping, restaurants and tourist attractions create an ideal location for a relaxing hospitality experience.

Walnut groves and oaks of the surrounding forests inspired the design. Organic building forms curve gently to reduce solar stress on all vertical surfaces. A replicating pattern of slender vertical windows and copper wall panels provides an abstract representation of

the crisscrossing furrows and ridges found in the bark of the walnut trees. These patterns rely on different window and wall panel types that are combined horizontally and vertically to provide a visually dynamic facade that is open to the north, tighter along the east and west sides, and shaded along the south.

The local beauty of the landscape inspired the warm palette of natural materials. Guests arrive at the lodge beneath a broad, cantilevered porte-cochère, then step into a welcoming space that features a canopy of wood extending from the ceiling. The wood surrounds an enormous hearth that anchors the lobby and bar. Glazed doors slide to seamlessly link the interior spaces with the adjacent terrace and entry courtyard.

With panoramic views of the surrounding hills, the rooftop level houses a ballroom,

meeting rooms, pre-function space, a lounge and a garden terrace. These open, connected spaces erase the boundaries between the interior and exterior environments.

◀ east view

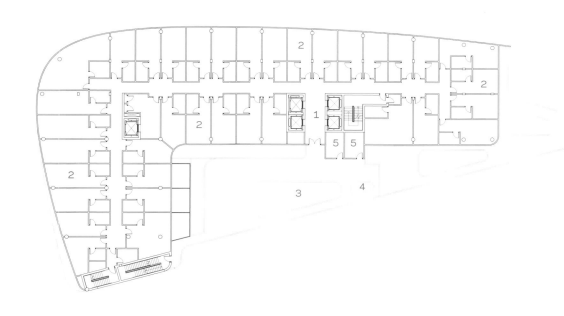

◄ level 3 floor plan

1 elevator lobby
2 guestrooms
3 pool
4 spa
5 restrooms

▼ ground level plan

1 lobby
2 restaurant + bar
3 kitchen
4 cafeteria
5 offices
6 storage + receiving

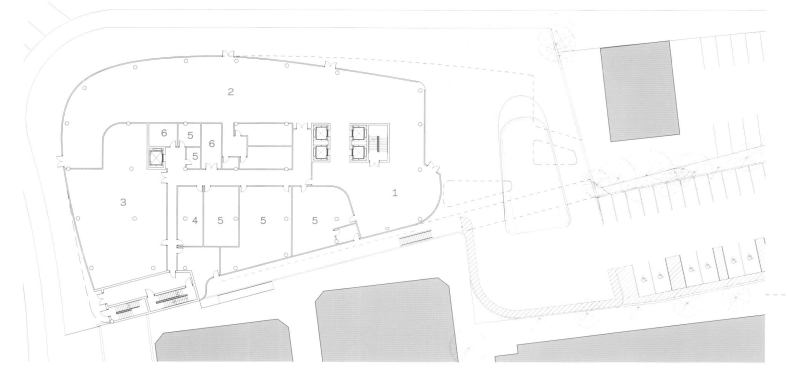

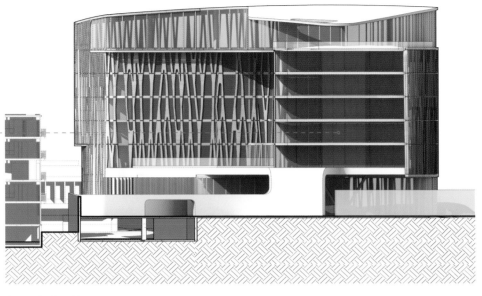

▲ south elevation

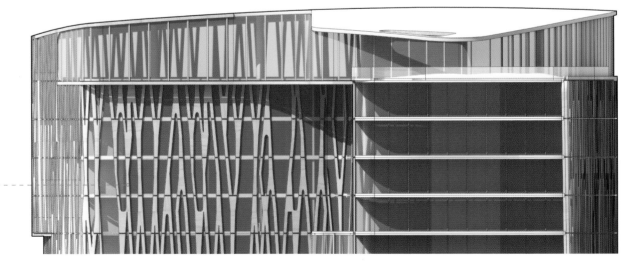

▲ east elevation

0
10
20

50

100ft

▲ main entrance

▲ view from northwest

▲ view from northeast

535 Mission Street
San Francisco, California, USA

354,000 sq. ft. / 32,900 sq. m.

Completion: 2014

The slender urban form of the 535 Mission Street tower is helping to transform the South of Market (SoMa) district of San Francisco.

Tapered facade corners and a sculptural cornice line define the 27-story building's silhouette. A double-height ground floor lobby, pedestrian plazas and improvements along Shaw Alley shape the street-level experience.

As one of the first LEED Core & Shell Gold pre-certified office towers in San Francisco, the building's advanced mechanical systems, high-performance skin and water-use efficiencies promote sustainability, occupant comfort and productivity. The facade features high-performance glass that integrates with indoor controls to enhance its energy and light transmission performance.

The project provides 3,700 square feet of ground-floor retail space to serve building occupants, visitors and city residents. The double-height lobby includes publicly accessible open space that flows into the covered outdoor plaza and features flexible seating, extensive landscaping and an espresso bar.

New trees and a continuous band of plantings along Shaw Alley soften the streetscape and enhance the pedestrian environment linking the building to the adjacent Transbay Terminal.

Concrete paving in the alley adds pedestrian scale and texture, establishing visual continuity.

◄ view from mission street

▶ ground level plan

1   mission street entry plaza
2   public plaza
3   lobby
4   retail + restaurant
5   elevator to high-rise
6   elevator to low-rise
7   service dock
8   ramp to basement parking

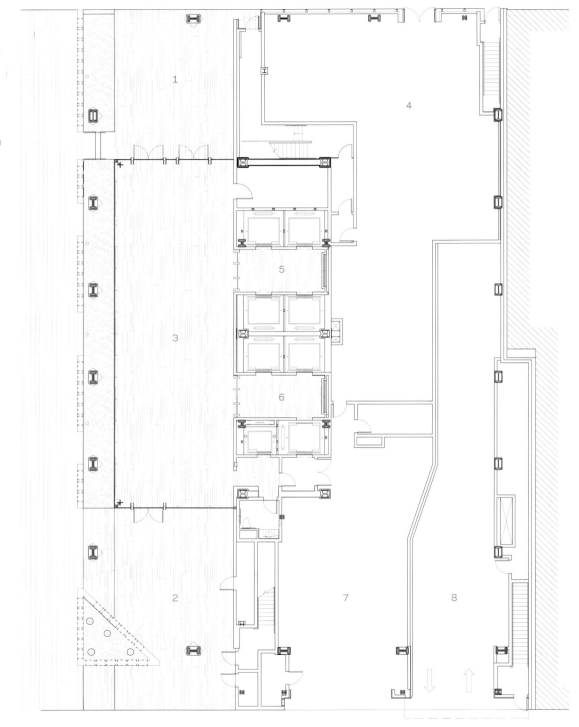

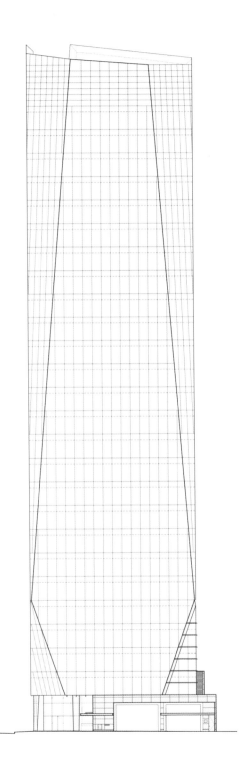

▲ southeast elevation

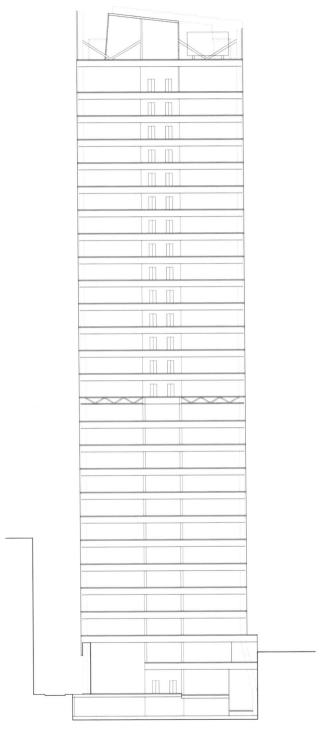

▲ section

▲ main entrance

▲ view from east

▲ main entrance from shaw alley

▲ lobby

535 MISSION STREET

National Center for Civil and Human Rights
Atlanta, Georgia, USA

42,000 sq. ft. / 3,900 sq. m.

Completion: 2014

Annual EUI: 87 kBTU / sf / yr
8.8% below national average

The concept of unity drove the design of Atlanta's National Center for Civil and Human Rights, which educates visitors about the rich history of the civil rights movement across the US while helping them connect lessons of the past to present-day issues.

Curved facades represent interlocking arms that cradle the central space, symbolizing unity and harmony. Inside, the three levels include exhibits and galleries, an event space, a broadcast studio and a retail store. The central open space was inspired by public areas in cities around the world in which protests for civil and human rights have taken place.

Moving through the building, visitors experience rich content through interactive exhibits and immersive activities. Though many of the issues explored are somber and difficult to discuss, the team designed the center to inspire conversation and action. Daylight floods the public spaces, including an overlook at the top of the central stair that serves as a spot for reflection.

Designed for LEED Gold certification, the building incorporates a high-performance exterior wall assembly, state-of-the-art environmental control systems, a vegetated roof and other energy-saving features.

HOK and the Freelon Group collaborated on the design of the building, which is in the heart of downtown Atlanta. Located a few blocks west of the Martin Luther King, Jr. National Historic Site, the museum is expected to draw 400,000 visitors annually.

◄ main entrance

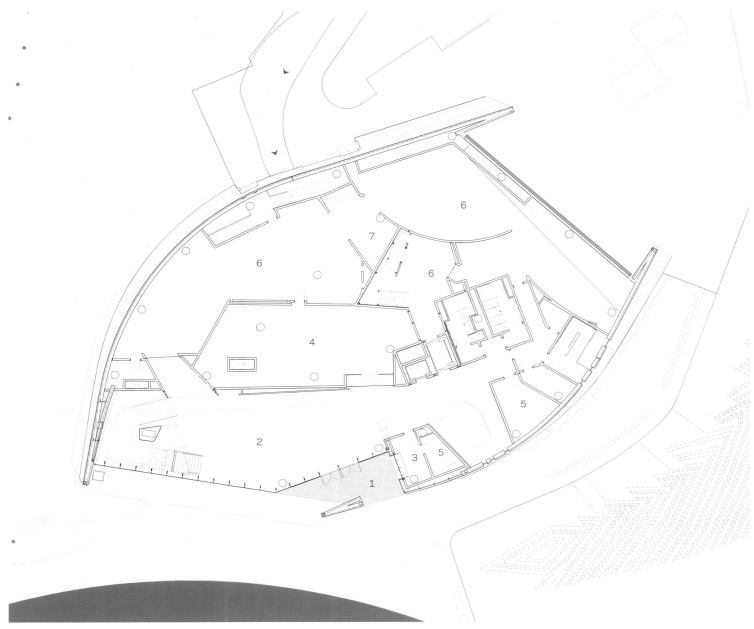

▲ ground level plan

1 main entrance
2 lobby
3 ticketing
4 gift shop
5 office
6 exhibit rooms
7 projector room

▲ sunshading

▲ main stair

▲ entrance lobby

0
5
10
20
40ft

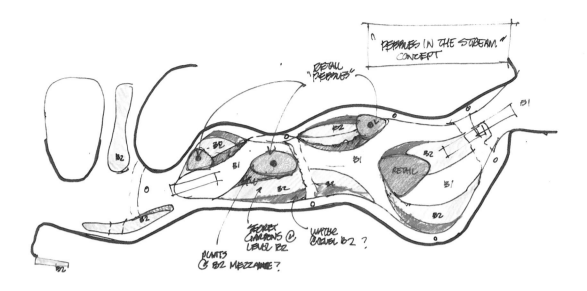

NEF Ataköy 22 Mixed-Use Development
Istanbul, Turkey

2.15 million sq. ft. / 200,000 sq. m.

Completion: 2017

This transit-oriented, mixed-use development in the Ataköy neighborhood of Istanbul features a community designed around six high-rise towers.

Developed by NEF Real Estate, the six-block site includes five 18-story residential towers housing 1,500 apartment and micro-apartment units, and a separate 18-story office tower. A shared podium connects the high-rises with a street-level retail mall that promotes pedestrian activity. Public transportation stations are located at each end of the development.

Because the site sits higher in the north than the south, the design provides a multi-level entry that creates a retail-office bridge between the two main roads.

Limestone, glass-fiber-reinforced concrete panels and ribbon windows on the residential towers create a modular, undulating facade

that accentuates the organic flow of the development and provides sunshading and visual harmony. Contrasting this curvilinear form, the podium-level garden apartments are housed in a faceted, zigzag massing that unifies individual tower blocks.

The towers are designed around a central square, allowing natural ventilation and light to the lower levels of the podium. Composed of unique gardens and pavilions, this multi-level linear courtyard promotes activity throughout the development. Bridges and walkways facilitate circulation and a sense of community.

Private residential terraces, plazas and roofscapes add garden spaces that provide visual continuity. Diverse residential amenities emphasize the social aspect of high-density living with a focus on entertainment and health — from private cinemas to basketball courts.

Building information modeling tools helped the design team maximize efficiencies. During the design phase, high market demand for residential units required one of the six towers originally designed for commercial office use to be redesigned as a residential tower in a compressed timeframe. The team also streamlined the constructability of the curvilinear concrete spandrel panels on four of the residential towers by devising a modular system that used a limited number of molds to create the complex forms seen throughout the development.

◀ pedestrian retail street

▲ north-south section

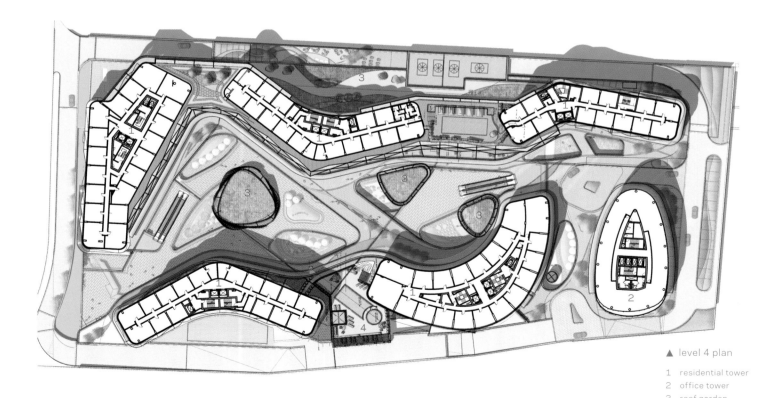

▲ level 4 plan

1   residential tower
2   office tower
3   roof garden
4   terrace

▲ aerial perspective

▲ facade diagram

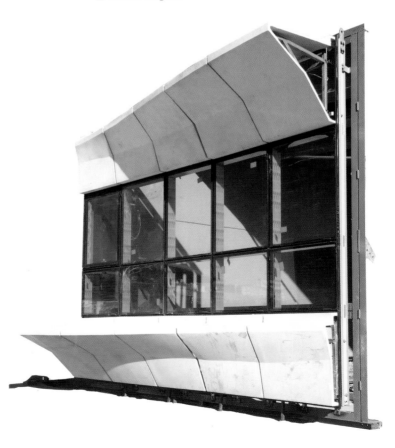

▲ facade mock-up

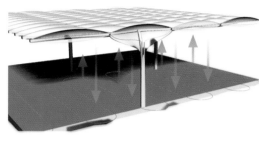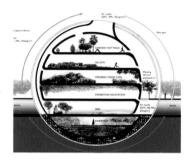

Net Zero Competition
Global

Competition: 2014

HOK's internal Net Zero Energy Design Competition challenged teams to create a conceptual net zero energy design for a site in their local community.

Specific urban infill sites were pre-selected in each office location. Entrants chose from four potential programs — medical office building, residential, commercial office building or academic building — with the ability to add retail and mixed-use components.

Teams were required to use HOK's Sustainable Analysis Tool to obtain climate data, set energy use intensity (EUI) targets and estimate the size of on-site renewable energy systems.

The design for the **SoLAr** mixed-use residential, commercial and retail project in Los Angeles integrates water, power and ventilation systems. Inspired by commercial installations in the Mojave Desert, the team designed a free-form veil with jewel-like concentrated photovoltaic (CPV) collectors. Heat generated by the CPV system can be used for solar water heating and geothermal

heating and cooling. As a semi-porous surface, the veil directs water runoff to filtration terraces for reuse.

For the **Feedback Hydronics** proposal, a fully integrated hydronic heating and cooling system powers a culinary school and restaurant in St. Louis. The system allows for feedback and self-correction while it adjusts operations in response to desired and actual outputs. Embedding a fully integrated solar thermal skin within the hydronic closed-loop system minimizes loss and maximizes gain. This quilt-like skin surface has four pod types for solar thermal collection, rainwater harvesting, photovoltaics and glazing. Secondary systems include a subterranean labyrinth, an anaerobic digester and an electronic chiller.

The **Urban Farm** proposal, a mixed-use commercial building and culinary school in Shanghai, generates energy through highly efficient systems that take advantage of the urban location. The building is divided into two volumes to separate energy generation from energy collection systems. Double-height

spaces accommodate urban farms that grow food. Photovoltaic panels on the facade capture solar energy, while a wind turbine generates wind energy.

The **D-Breath** medical office building in Beijing features a passive ventilation system that purifies and filters the air, helping to mitigate air pollution in the region. An intelligent, charcoal-brick framework and infill system incorporate smart modules. The system harvests solar heat for energy exchange. Natural ventilation strategies are integrated into the structure and envelope. Customizing the infill system to the specific geographic location maximizes the building's performance and gives the design flexibility to adapt to different locations across the world.

◄ solar view from southeast

solar: los angeles, california, usa

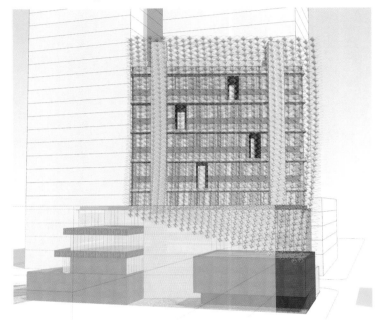

▲ south elevation

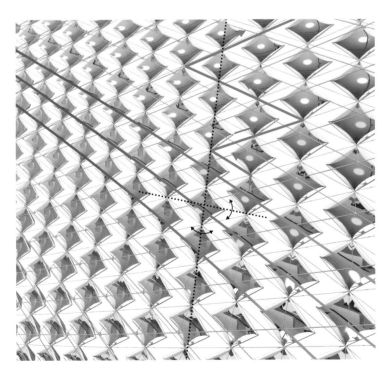

▲ facade detail

▲ site plan

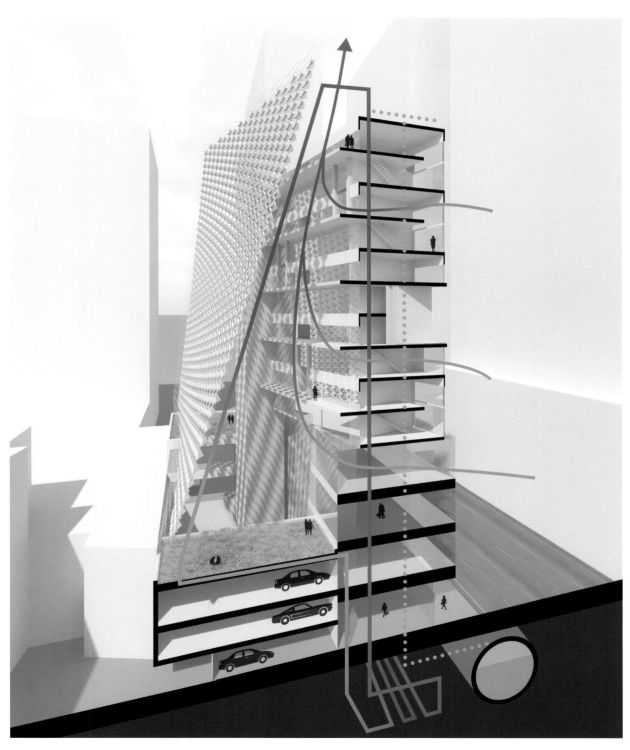

▲ section perspective

feedback hydronics: st. louis, missouri, usa

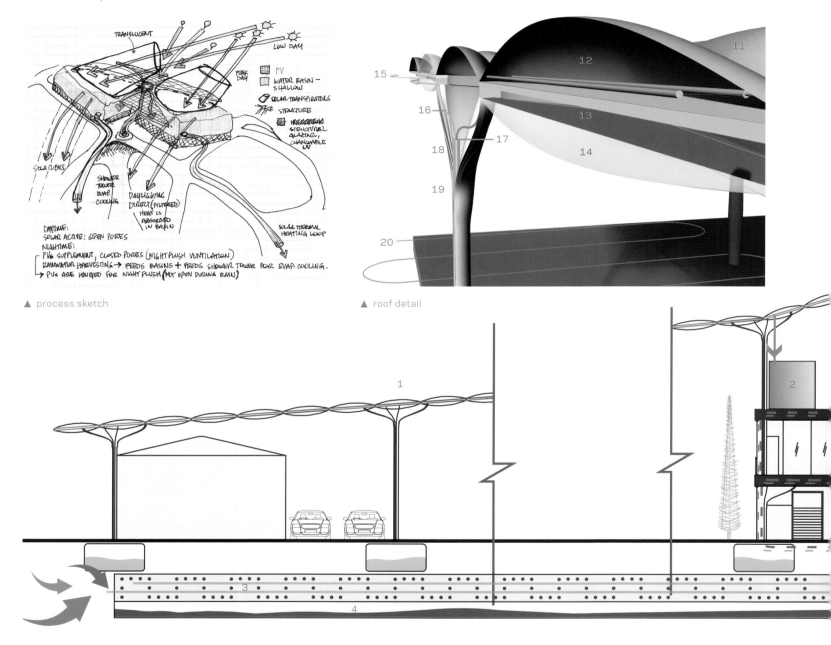

▲ process sketch

▲ roof detail

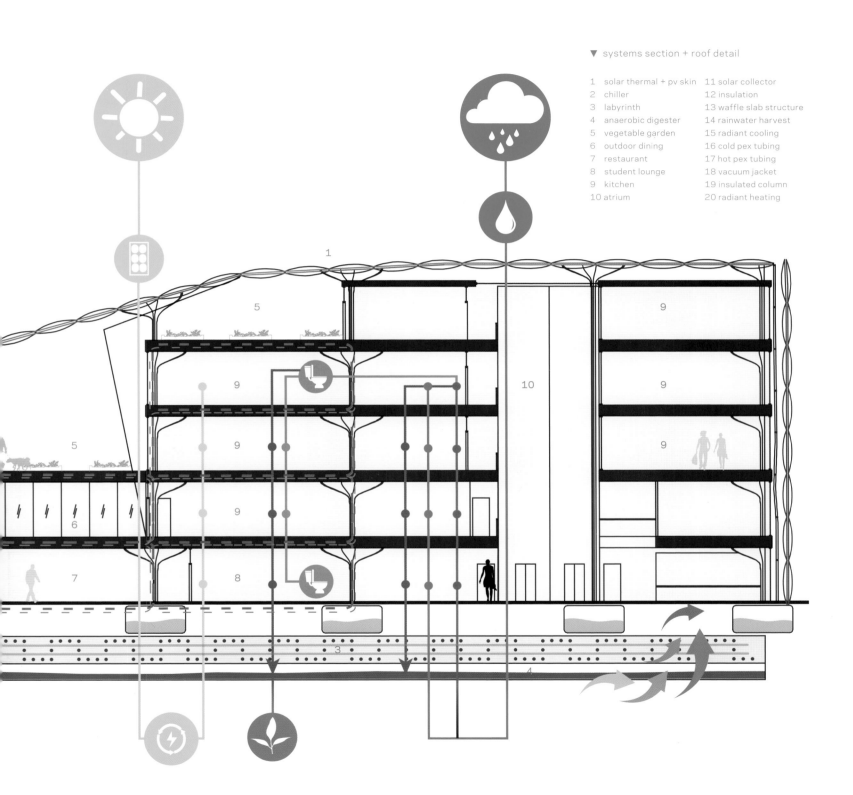

▼ systems section + roof detail

1	solar thermal + pv skin	11	solar collector
2	chiller	12	insulation
3	labyrinth	13	waffle slab structure
4	anaerobic digester	14	rainwater harvest
5	vegetable garden	15	radiant cooling
6	outdoor dining	16	cold pex tubing
7	restaurant	17	hot pex tubing
8	student lounge	18	vacuum jacket
9	kitchen	19	insulated column
10	atrium	20	radiant heating

urban farm: shanghai, china

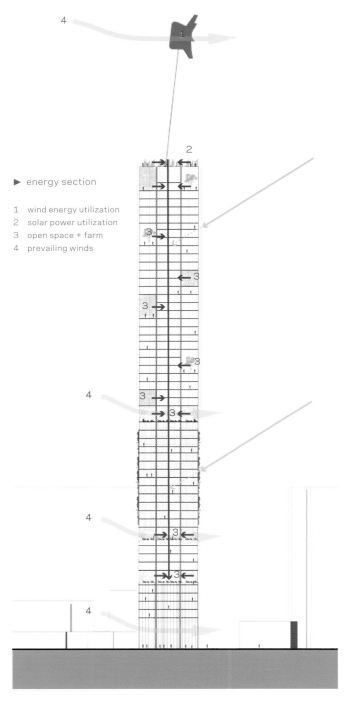

► energy section

1 wind energy utilization
2 solar power utilization
3 open space + farm
4 prevailing winds

▲ context: shanghai

▲ rendering

d-breath: beijing, china

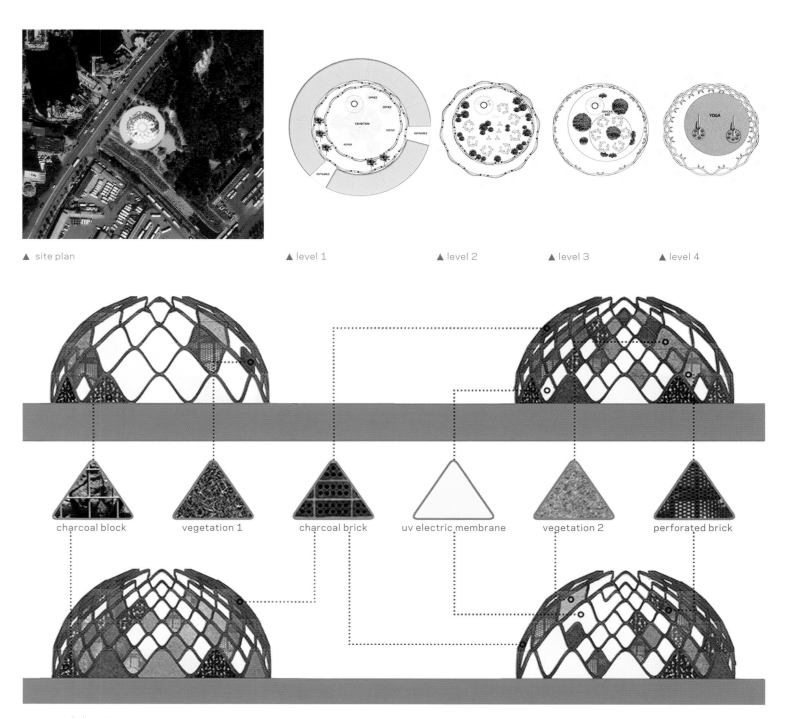

▲ site plan   ▲ level 1   ▲ level 2   ▲ level 3   ▲ level 4

charcoal block   vegetation 1   charcoal brick   uv electric membrane   vegetation 2   perforated brick

▲ material elevations

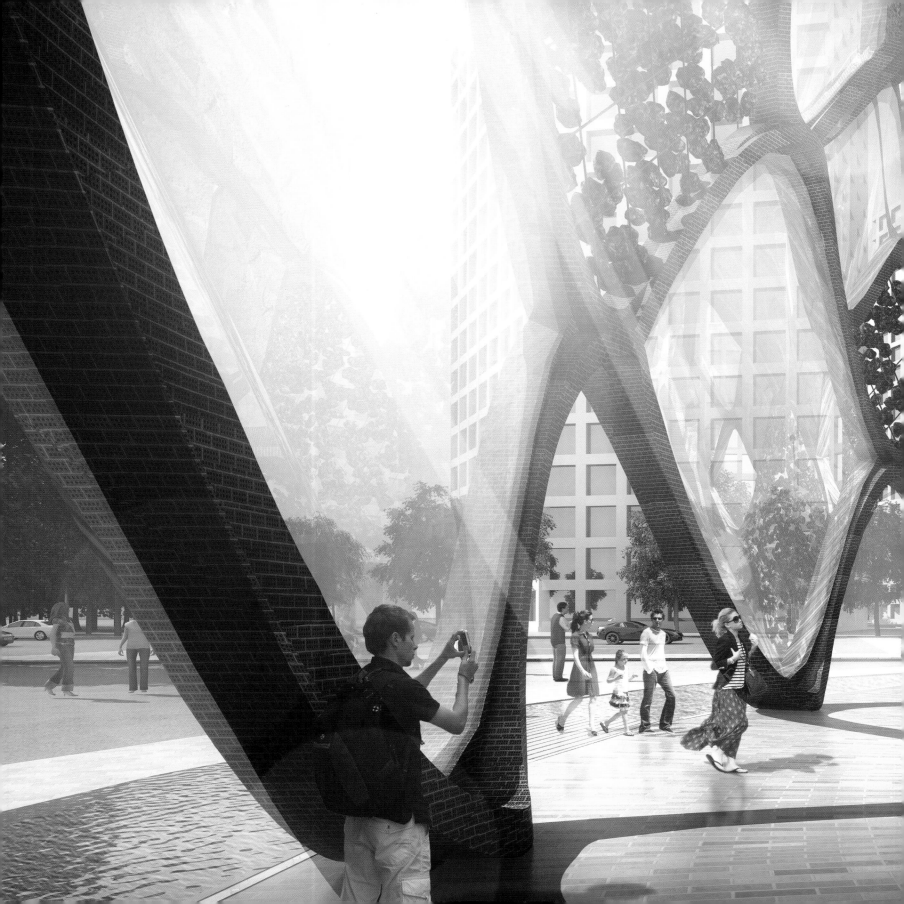

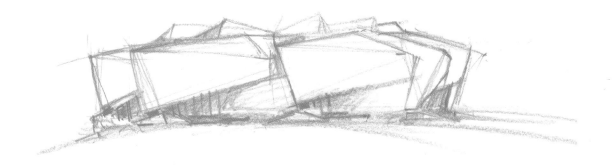

New Atlanta Stadium
Atlanta, Georgia, USA

2 million sq. ft. / 185,800 sq. m.

**Seats: 71,000 for NFL games /
32,456 for MLS games**

Completion: 2017

The design of the New Atlanta Stadium creates an exceptional game-day experience for fans and an iconic architectural landmark for the city.

Designed as a signature element rather than a utilitarian cover, the New Atlanta Stadium's retractable roof provides a radical departure from the kinetic roofs of other sports facilities. Derived from the shape of a falcon's wing, a reference to the Atlanta Falcons National Football League team, the roof features eight triangular panels that wrap the stadium and move in unison along individual tracks. This allows the roof to open and close like a camera aperture. Exterior lighting can easily change the color of the transparent facade.

The stadium interior offers fans an immersive, technology-driven game-day experience. A wide variety of seating options provide fans with different ticket prices, vantage points, degrees of service and amenities. A 360-degree HD halo video board built into the roof offers clear views from every seat. Other amenities include a technology lounge, a 100-yard bar and floor-to-ceiling windows offering views of downtown Atlanta.

Designed for flexibility, the stadium can be quickly reconfigured to accommodate games for Atlanta's new Major League Soccer franchise. Retractable seats surrounding the field allow fans to get close to the action for both football and soccer. Digital media

platforms throughout the stadium offer flexible opportunities for teams and sponsors to display targeted programmable content on game days.

In addition to serving as an anchor for the downtown tourist and entertainment district, the stadium will catalyze changes in neighborhoods surrounding the development. The project team's focus on sustainable design, construction and operations extends into the community through the creation of urban farms and open recreation spaces.

HOK is collaborating on the design with tvsdesign, Goode Van Slyke Architecture and Stanley Beaman & Sears.

◄ stadium interior

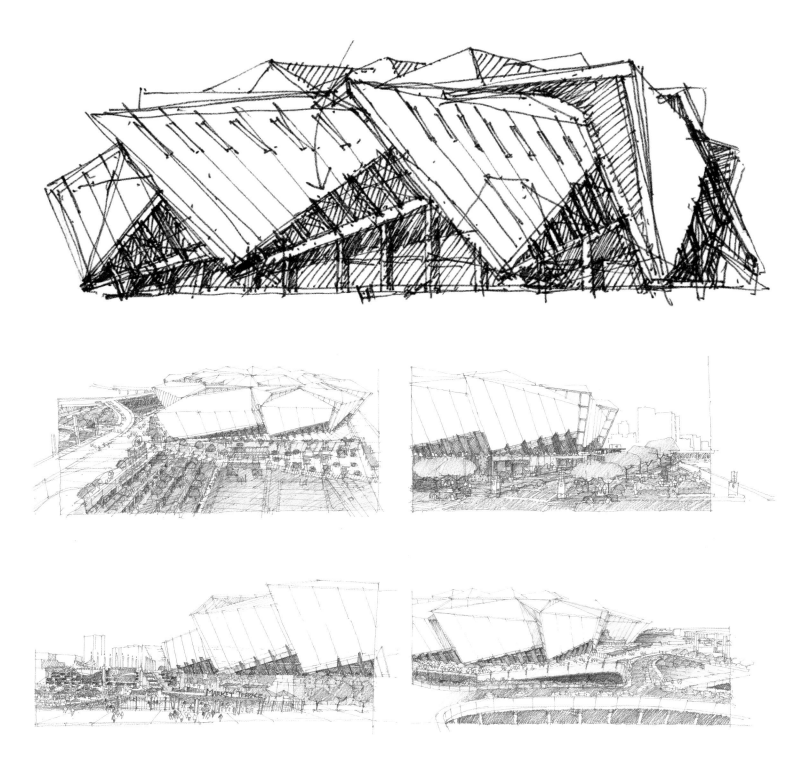

▲ concept sketches

▲ transparent facade

▲ window to the city

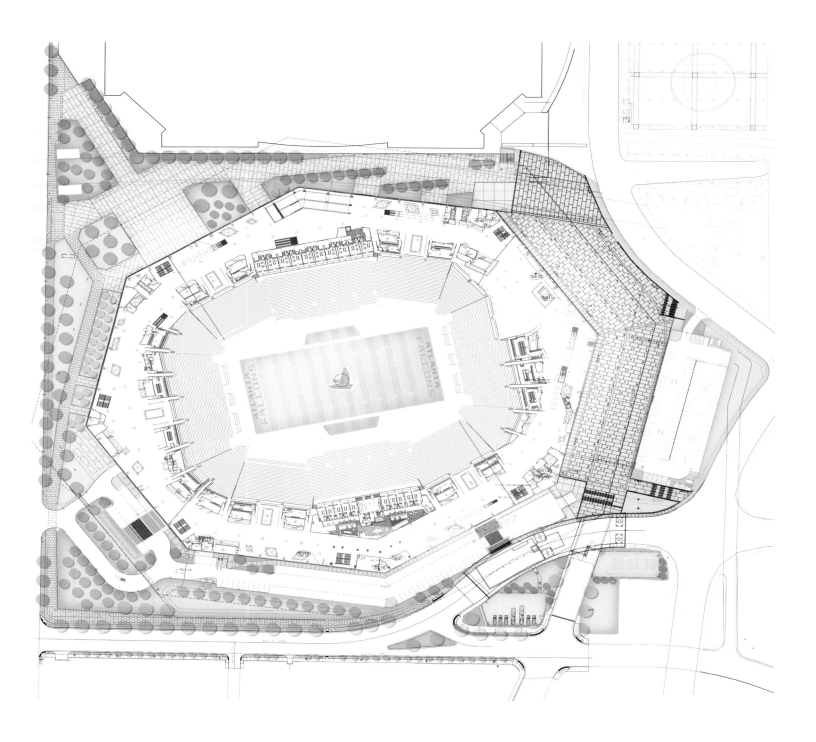

▲ site plan

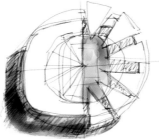
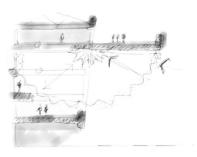

▲ concept sketches

0
50
100
200
400ft

▲ entry plaza at falcons landing

The New York Palace Hotel Suites and Lounges
New York, New York, USA

Champagne Suite: 4,620 sq. ft. / 430 sq. m.
Jewel Suite: 4,000 sq. ft. / 370 sq. m.
Tavern on 51: 1,390 sq. ft. / 130 sq. m.
Rarities: 1,440 sq. ft. / 135 sq. m.

Completion: 2013

Two luxurious suites and two premier lounges help the historic New York Palace distinguish itself from other five-star properties.

The multi-level **Champagne Suite** combines modern and classic elements to create a glamorous penthouse space. Guests encounter a striking series of floor-to-ceiling windows that flood the grand parlor with natural light while offering breathtaking views of Manhattan.

Polished marble and rustic stone pay tribute to champagne cellars. A custom-designed chandelier of multicolored handblown glass provides a focal point. A double-story wall is adorned with a black-and-white mural depicting a hillside medieval abbey and the town where champagne originated.

Influenced by the Chardonnay grape, the master bedroom's décor features a palette of ecru, cream and amber tones. The guest bedroom suite draws inspiration from the more intense notes of a Pinot Noir, featuring rose-tinted silvers with warm copper and deep red accents.

Created with jewelry designer Martin Katz, the **Jewel Suite** merges romance, abstract elements of nature and Art Deco-inspired details in one luxurious setting. Guests experience a grand staircase, lavish Port Laurent stone floors, diamond-like wall coverings, a 20-foot diamond waterfall chandelier and floating crystal jewel boxes encasing jewelry creations designed by Katz. The sprawling grand parlor is flooded with light from the suite's floor-to-ceiling windows.

These themes continue on the second floor, where luxuriant sleeping spaces provide an intimate retreat and a presentation room accommodates guests who want to try on jewelry. The romantic environment soars to new heights on the suite's third floor, which features an antique Louis XIV-style Carrara marble mantel and a wood-burning fireplace.

The inspiration behind **Tavern on 51** is derived from the Villard Mansion, the classic 19th-century residence of railroad mogul Henry Villard housed within the hotel. The design features a combination of colors and fabrics that evoke elegance rooted in turn-of-the-century charm and authenticity.

Accessible from 51st Street and the hotel, the cocktail lounge offers a posh yet relaxed atmosphere. Historic elements are embellished with modern touches, perfect for visitors seeking a spirited yet intimate atmosphere. A magnificent stained glass window is accented by carefully selected modern oil paintings and sconces.

The exclusive **Rarities** lounge features premium select liquors in a members-only setting. Transformed from a former meeting space, the two-room venue includes a connecting hall and landmark stairwell featuring 30-to-40-foot vaulted ceilings, detailed millwork, cove windows and fireplaces.

Discreet antique embellishments and re-upholstered walls blend with the fireplace and other historic elements. Using rich damasks and a burgundy and aubergine palette, luxurious old-world style is enriched with new carpet, case goods and a mix of furniture and soft goods. To maintain an authentic feel, the team sourced digital reproductions and frames to complement original oil portraits and prints.

◄ jewel suite living room

champagne suite level 2 ▶

1 master bedroom
2 master bathroom
3 library
4 bathroom
5 second bedroom

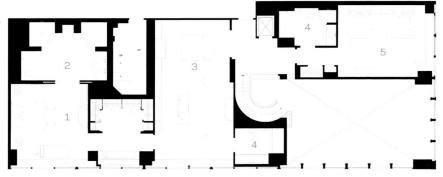

bedroom textures

▲ champagne suite living room

▲ champagne suite library

▲ bedroom textures

jewel suite level 2 ▶

1 master bedroom
2 master bathroom
3 boudoir
4 bathroom
5 second bedroom

▲ jewel suite office

▲ jewel suite rooftop

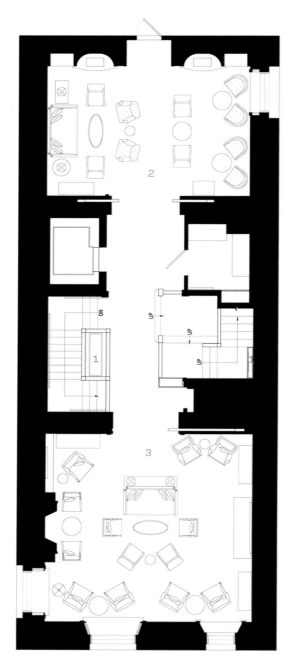

▲ rarities plan

1 display
2 empire room
3 red room

▲ rarities display

▲ tavern 51 bar

NOAA Inouye Regional Center
Pearl Harbor, Hawaii, USA

350,000 sq. ft. / 32,515 sq. m.

Completion: 2014

32.7% below ASHRAE 2007

Located on a national historic landmark site on Oahu's Ford Island, the National Oceanic and Atmospheric Administration (NOAA) Inouye Regional Center features the adaptive reuse of two World War II-era airplane hangars linked by a new steel and glass building. The original aircraft hangars, designed in 1939 by Albert Kahn, inspired beautifully simple solutions for how the new center uses air, water and light.

The complex accommodates 800 people in a high-performance research and office campus that integrates NOAA's mission of "science, service and stewardship" with the region's cultural traditions and the island's ecology. It houses a diverse range of critical programs, functions and federal departments, including the Pacific Tsunami Warning Center.

Facilities include wet and dry research laboratories, a marine center, a library, administrative offices, conference and meeting areas, a dining hall and informal collaboration spaces.

The interior environment is based on the principles of campus design. Creating a central gathering place, the plan supports program-intensive workplaces with internal quadrangles of open space with primary and secondary circulation routes.

Connecting the front door of the campus with the waterfront, the three-story atrium knits together a sequence of materials and volumetric plane changes to give people a sense of progression as they move through the building. A series of interactive exhibits highlight the history of the island and region, as well as NOAA's diverse mission.

Located at the northern end of the atrium, the dining hall provides users with a panoramic view to the water and the mountain range in the distance. The fully glazed two-story space maximizes transparency and creates a fluid visual experience. A 200-seat auditorium provides tiered seating for NOAA programs, while multiple conference rooms and flexible classrooms support collaborative activities.

The biological influences of the region guided the design of the anticipated LEED Gold project. A skylight diffuser system virtually eliminates the need for artificial light during the day. Hawaii's first hydronic passive cooling unit (PCU) system uses chilled water from a nearby building and natural ventilation to condition the space through an underground air distribution system. A graywater capturing system is used to irrigate the native landscaping.

◀ atrium

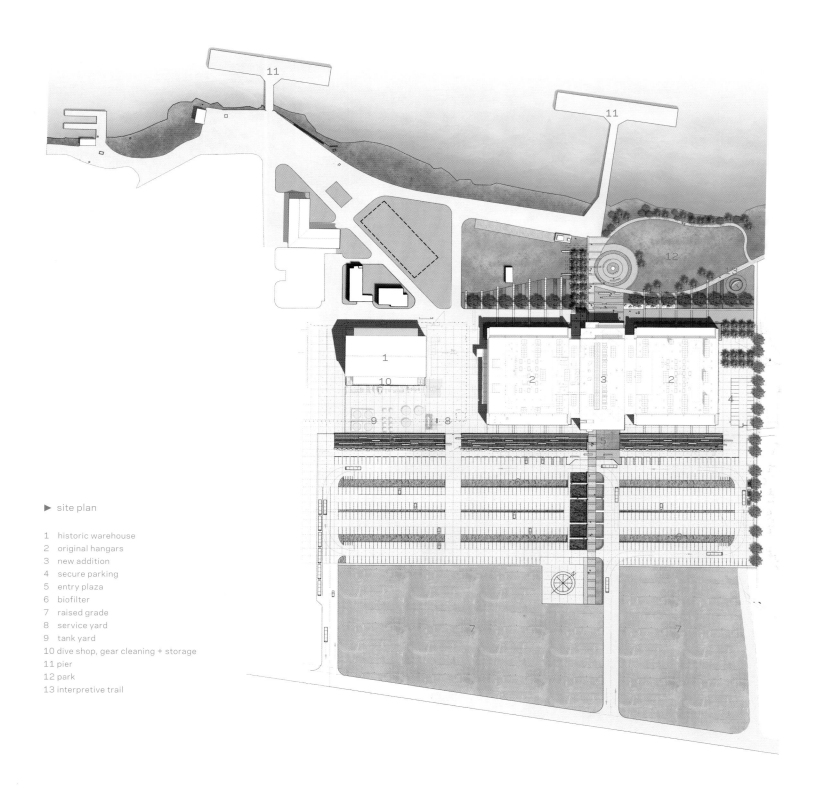

► site plan

1 historic warehouse
2 original hangars
3 new addition
4 secure parking
5 entry plaza
6 biofilter
7 raised grade
8 service yard
9 tank yard
10 dive shop, gear cleaning + storage
11 pier
12 park
13 interpretive trail

▲ interior before renovation   ▲ internal courtyard

0
20
50
100
150ft

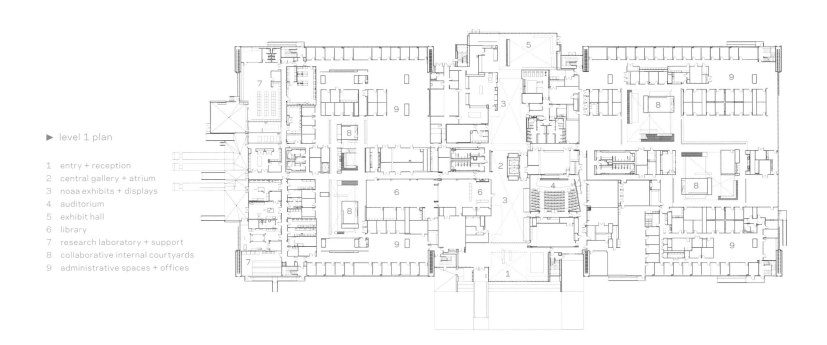

► level 1 plan

1 entry + reception
2 central gallery + atrium
3 noaa exhibits + displays
4 auditorium
5 exhibit hall
6 library
7 research laboratory + support
8 collaborative internal courtyards
9 administrative spaces + offices

▲ daylighting studies

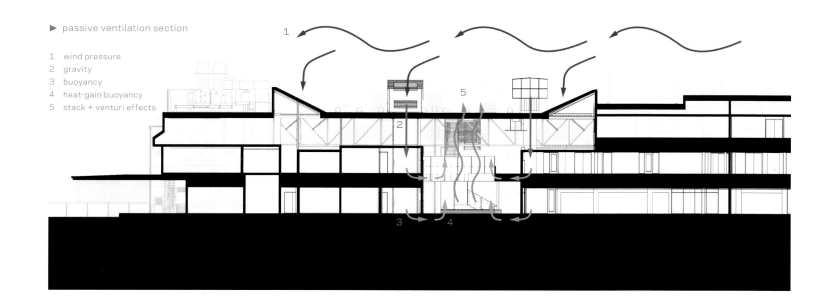

▶ passive ventilation section

1 wind pressure
2 gravity
3 buoyancy
4 heat-gain buoyancy
5 stack + venturi effects

▲ internal courtyard concept

▲ internal courtyard realization

▲ exhibit hall

▲ south entry

▲ north entry

▲ dining hall

▲ dining hall sunshading

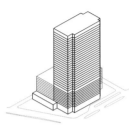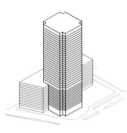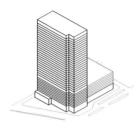

Office Building Design Competition
Houston, Texas, USA

620,000 sq. ft. / 57,600 sq. m.

Competition: 2014

The design for this office building, centrally located within Houston's prominent Uptown District, complements the dynamic urban neighborhood.

Home to more than 180,000 residents and 28 million square feet of office space within a three-mile radius, Houston's Uptown District is known for its "live, work, shop" lifestyle.

Situated directly adjacent to Houston's light rail line, the three-acre parcel provides access to The Galleria, Memorial Park, Hermann Park and the Houston Medical Center. Each proposed design scenario focuses on maximizing visibility while helping to define the downtown Houston landscape.

The 24-story tower has an innovative curtain wall system featuring transparent, full-height vision glass, spandrel glass, a reflective glazing system and exterior sun control

devices. The facade provides solar protection and privacy while allowing for large expanses of floor-to-ceiling glass.

Nearly 90,000 square feet of amenity space includes a grand lobby designed to reflect the aesthetics of a world-renowned hotel. Ground-floor retail space, a conference center and a fitness facility support the developer's goal of attracting and retaining tenants by promoting work-life balance.

A 12-level (two floors below grade and 10 floors above grade) parking podium features a rooftop terrace offering views of downtown.

The design preserves many existing large trees, integrating the tower into the surrounding landscape and creating a lush canopy for the enjoyment of tenants and pedestrians.

◄ view from southeast

▲ site plan

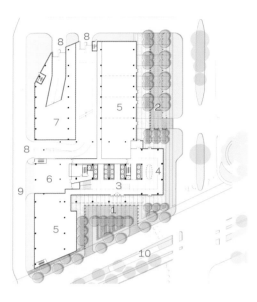

► ground floor plan

1 drop-off
2 retail access
3 main office lobby
4 urban room
5 retail
6 loading dock
7 central plant
8 garage access
9 service
10 light rail platform

▲ south elevation

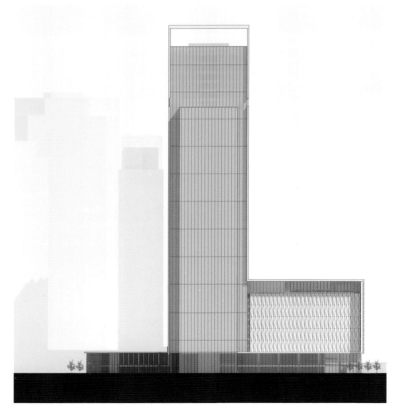

▲ east elevation

▲ interior atrium + lobby

0
40
80
120
200ft

The Ohio State University Comprehensive Cancer Center
James Cancer Hospital and Solove Research Institute
Columbus, Ohio, USA

1.1 million sq. ft. / 102,000 sq. m.

Completion: 2014

As the country's third-largest cancer hospital, Ohio State's James Cancer Hospital and Solove Research Institute (OSUCCC — James) serves as an innovative model for 21st-century hospitals devoted to cancer care.

The 21-level, 306-bed freestanding cancer hospital brings together clinical care, research and education in a highly subspecialized care model called precision cancer medicine.

Each inpatient unit has its own cancer focus, such as gastrointestinal, head and neck, breast, genitourinary or hematologic malignancies. The oncologists, nurses, pharmacists and genomic experts on each unit treat only that type of cancer. Medical staff collaborate with researchers to examine every patient's genes and tumor DNA to determine the best treatment and accelerate research discoveries. Translational research labs on each inpatient floor bring physicians and researchers together to develop and deliver targeted treatments.

A cancer emergency department — one of only a few in the US — is integrated with The Ohio State University Wexner Medical Center's main emergency department and includes 15 cancer treatment stations staffed by doctors and nurses specially trained in oncology and emergency medicine.

The center's extensive cancer surgical facilities house 14 operating rooms, including six interventional operating suites and two suites connected to a 3-Tesla MRI, allowing patients to be imaged during surgery. Intraoperative radiation therapy and MRI technologies offer surgeons more precise diagnostics and treatment options.

Natural light is a key design feature throughout the hospital. An above-ground radiation oncology center with seven treatment vaults is located on the hospital's second floor, providing access to natural light and views overlooking a park.

Patients, visitors and staff can enjoy outdoor cafés and terrace gardens on the 14th floor, where plantings include vegetables with cancer-preventive properties.

To enhance safety, all private inpatient rooms feature identical layouts. Sophisticated technology supports patient care and entertainment, while large windows offer expansive views. Hotel-like amenities accommodate families and visitors. Each floor also integrates visitor lounges, consultation rooms, Wi-Fi capabilities and respite areas.

◀ patient drop-off entrance

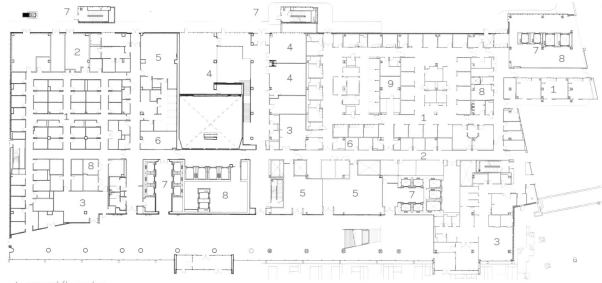

▲ ground floor plan

1 exam + consultation   4 conference room   7 vertical circulation
2 lounge + office   5 lab   8 mechanical room
3 public + family waiting area   6 pharmacy   9 storage

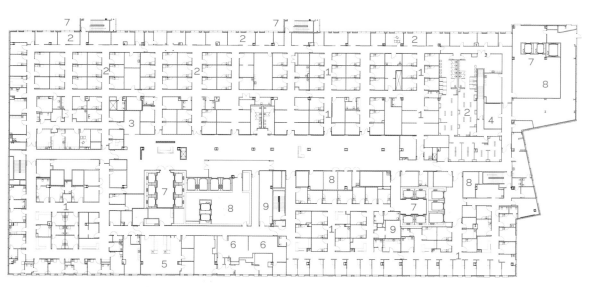

▲ level 5 floor plan

1 patient rooms   4 conference room   7 vertical circulation
2 lounge + office   5 lab   8 mechanical room
3 public + family waiting area   6 pharmacy   9 storage

▲ grand staircase in main lobby

0 10 20   50   100ft

▲ facade overall view

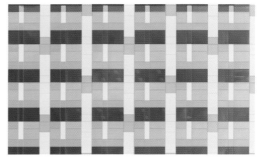

▲ spandrel glass

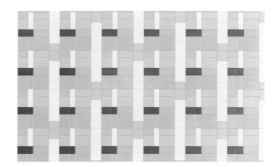

▲ vision glass

3'-10"   3'-10"   3'-10"   3'-10"

5

1

4'-0"

3

2'-8"

2

2'-8"

2'-8"

4

2'-8"

► facade organization

1 spandrel glass
2 vision glass
3 frosted glass
4 fritted glass
5 metal panel

▲ frosted glass

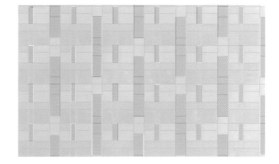

▲ metal panel

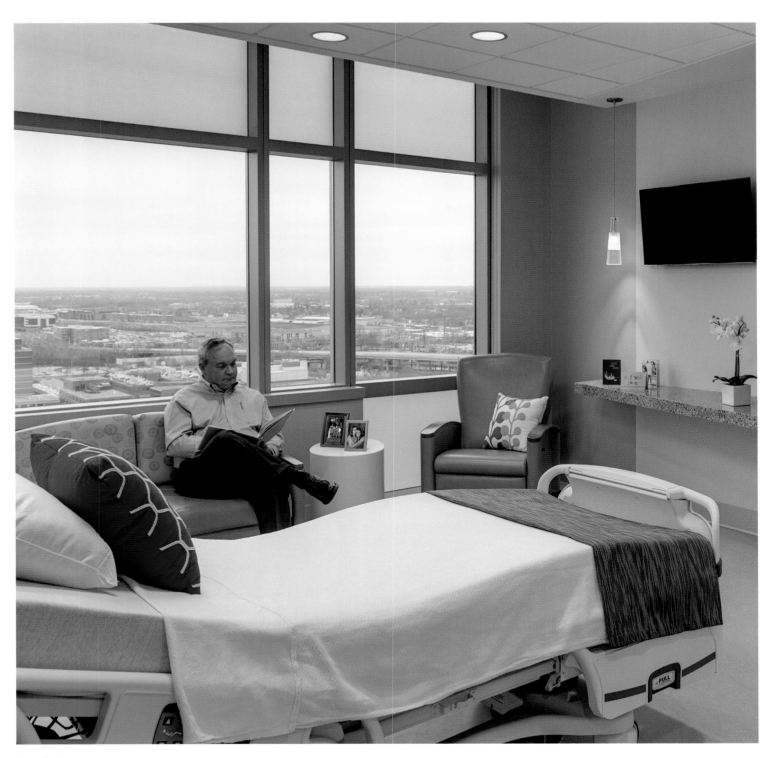

▲ patient room

OpenText Toronto Executive Offices
Toronto, Ontario, Canada

20,500 sq. ft. / 1,900 sq. m.

Completion: 2014

The design of state-of-the-art executive offices and a client briefing center for Canada's largest software company reflects the firm's innovative culture.

Located on the top two floors of a downtown Toronto office tower, OpenText's new office space accommodates visiting executives, clients and permanent staff. The 12th floor houses a reception area, executive visitor meeting center and offices for resident senior executives.

A central staircase connects to the 11th floor, which includes other private offices, collaborative work areas and benching workstations to support the 48-person staff.

Distinctive circular domed ceilings with elegant skylights offer dramatic detailing and ample daylight. One dome is located over the executive boardroom at the north end of the floor and another is at the south end above the client briefing center and kitchenette.

The design team implemented advanced display and technology systems to support client presentations. Custom curved millwork units house the display screens in the boardroom and client briefing center. An LED video wall in the reception area showcases OpenText's expertise, practice areas and values.

Other contemporary design features include geometric light fixtures, modern office furniture and vibrant carpets.

◄ executive boardroom

▲ interconnecting stair + reception waiting area

▲ executive boardroom

▲ executive office

Patricia Louise Frost Music Studios
Miami, Florida, USA

New construction:
41,000 sq. ft. / 3,800 sq. m.

Renovation:
20,000 sq. ft. / 1,860 sq. m.

Completion: 2015

Annual EUI north wing: 83 kBTU / sf / yr
36% energy reduction from average

Annual EUI south wing: 64 kBTU / sf / yr
38% energy reduction from average

The Patricia Louise Frost Music Studios complex is the first phase of a master plan to renovate and expand the Frost School of Music on the University of Miami's campus.

The plan, which will add 86,000 square feet of new space to the heart of the campus, includes the construction of four new buildings and the renovation of four existing mid-century modern structures. It also creates a new courtyard and preserves green space within the central quadrangle.

Framed in structural white precast concrete, the Patricia Louise Frost Music Studios complex is designed to maximize natural light and views while minimizing solar heat gain and glare.

Each of the 77 chamber-music studios is a "floating box-within-a-box," with independent walls, floors and ceilings to provide optimal acoustics for teaching, learning and performing music. The facility also includes two oversized rehearsal halls, a reception and information center, and a furnished breezeway.

Designed for LEED Platinum certification, the complex integrates energy-efficient windows, rooftop solar panels and water cisterns.

The next phase of the master plan will include a state-of-the-art, 200-seat recital hall with a glass-backed performance stage that overlooks Lake Osceola and its central fountain.

Future phases will create another teaching building and the Center for Experiential Music, which will contain classrooms, mixing and control rooms, a jazz rehearsal room, and two performance spaces: the "White Box" recital hall for pure acoustic performance and practice and the "Black Box" recital hall for mixed media, electronic music, performance and experimentation.

All new buildings are being designed with careful attention to the unique acoustic requirements. Existing buildings will be carefully renovated and modernized to respect their historic value.

◄ new gateway entrance

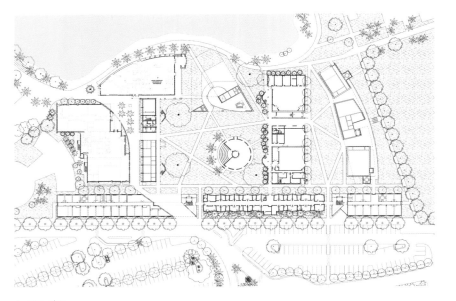

▲ site plan

▲ stair detail

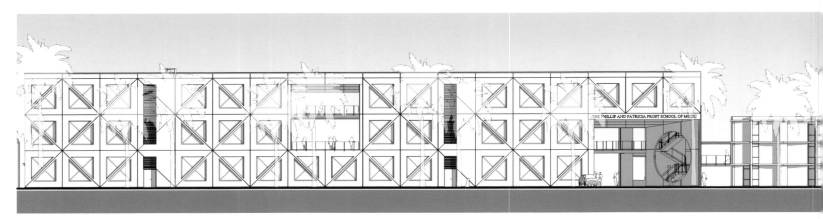

▲ phase 1 elevation

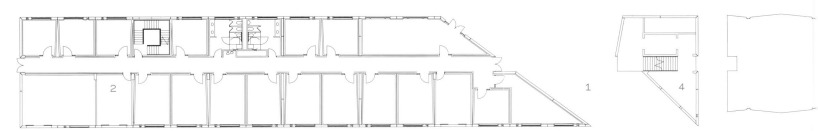

▲ ground level floor plan

1 school of music gateway
2 typical music studios
3 existing foster building
4 vertical circulation
5 percussion studio

▲ street view looking southwest

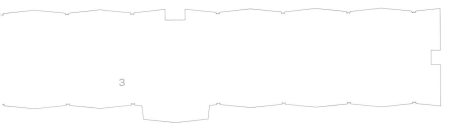

3

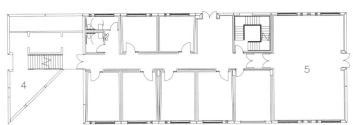

4

5

▲ percussion rehearsal room

Polsinelli Headquarters
Kansas City, Missouri, USA

Office building:
225,000 sq. ft. / 20,900 sq. m.

Plaza Vista mixed-use development:
250,000 sq. ft. / 23,225 sq. m.

Completion: 2013

The new headquarters for Polsinelli gives this fast-growing law firm a signature office building that embodies its culture and values.

As the anchor tenant of the Plaza Vista mixed-use development, Polsinelli had clear goals for the building's interior environment and architectural character. The team worked closely with the law firm's leaders and developer VanTrust Real Estate to design a building that achieved Polsinelli's vision while creating a valuable asset for VanTrust.

Designed to showcase views of Country Club Plaza, the interior environment for Polsinelli's 450 employees is timeless and metropolitan. A seven-story, cantilevered stairwell winds through the center of the building and acts like a sculptural wood ribbon that creates visual and physical connectivity. As the primary architectural element in the space, the stairwell provides a graceful elegance that balances the rectilinear forms of the building.

The plan's strategic adjacencies optimize operational efficiencies and give Polsinelli the flexibility to reconfigure the layout over its 20-year lease. The team paid close attention to the size and allocation of offices, libraries, attorney lounges and other ancillary areas.

Polsinelli's modern work environment features collaborative seating areas throughout the building and sit-stand workstations in all administrative and associate offices. Multipurpose training rooms provide space for mock trials, while the attorney lounge provides flexible seating options.

The LEED certified building features an H-shaped footprint composed of two precast and glass structures connected by a central glass link. The massing of the structure reduces the building's visual scale, creates outdoor spaces at the entries and maximizes the number of offices along the windows. Vertical proportions and a distinct precast texture pay homage to the surrounding Country Club Plaza architecture.

◀ central stair

▲ level 9 terrace

▲ reception

▲ level 4 stair

▲ attorney lounge

7 West Conference

Break Room

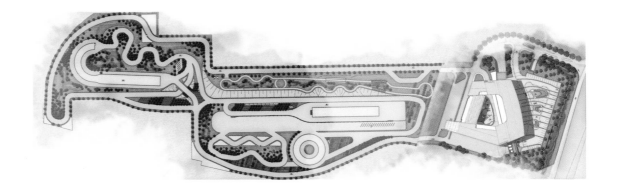

Porsche Cars North America Experience Center and Headquarters
Atlanta, Georgia, USA

260,000 sq. ft. / 24,160 sq. m.

Completion: 2015

The design of Porsche's new experience center and headquarters combines office, training and driving functions into one sleek, high-performance facility that encapsulates the essence of the company's brand.

Bringing together 450 Porsche employees from five divisions of the company, the facility serves as a new destination for partners, customers and car enthusiasts.

An estimated 30,000 guests are expected to visit the Porsche Experience Center (PEC) each year. By integrating a 1.6-mile driver track into the lower levels of the office building and weaving in subtle motor-sport-related cues, the design immerses employees and visitors in the Porsche experience while demonstrating the unique capabilities of its sports cars. The track, which runs through

the facility's courtyard, includes six driving modules designed to demonstrate the capabilities of different Porsche models. Classic and modern Porsches are on display in a classic car gallery.

Visitors can see historic Porsches undergoing renovations with vintage German parts at the restoration center. In the design studio, customers can virtually create their dream cars with fully customizable options. Restaurant 356, named after the first production Porsche, offers diners a front row seat to the test track. The center also includes a driving simulator lab.

Designed for LEED Silver certification, the building's east-west exposures eliminate glare. The north-south curtain walls maximize natural light and minimize solar heat gain.

The contemporary, naturally illuminated office space encourages collaboration and creativity among Porsche staff. A 13,000-sq.-ft. business center features state-of-the-art conference rooms and event spaces.

Located on a former automobile production facility adjacent to Hartsfield-Jackson Atlanta International Airport, the building and test track are a prominent symbol of the Porsche brand to passengers on arriving and departing flights. The facility is expected to catalyze development in the burgeoning aerotropolis.

◄ view to north entry

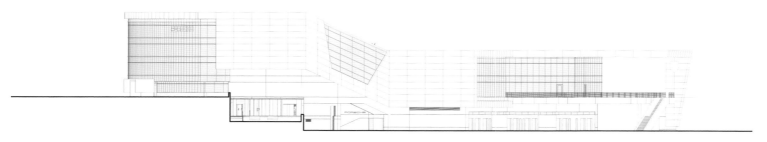

▲ west elevation

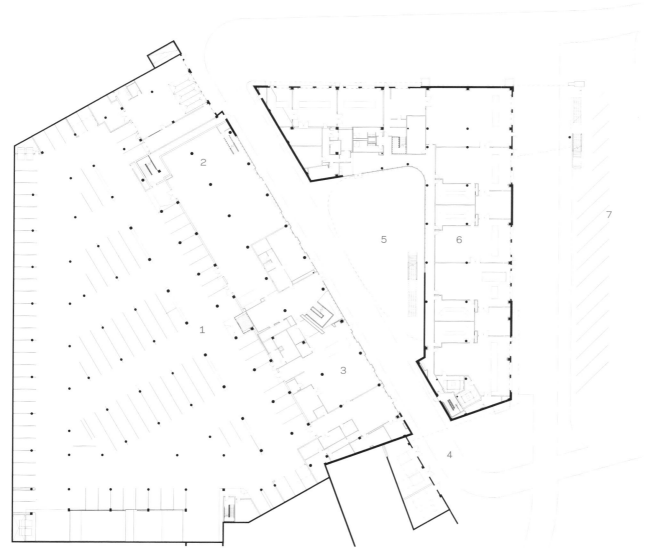

◄ track level 1

1 employee parking
2 heritage center
3 classic restoration
4 drive track
5 courtyard
6 technical training
7 pit lane
8 business center
9 outdoor terrace
10 headquarters zone
11 experience center
12 business center
13 employee cafeteria
14 356 restaurant
15 roof terrace

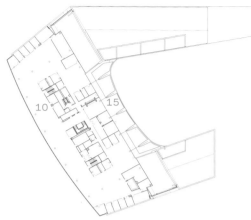

▲ level 5 plan

▲ level 4 plan

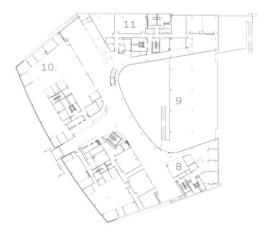

▲ level 3 plan

▲ vehicular access through building

▲ view of driving track + courtyard

▲ car display + gift shop

▲ view of the east elevation

  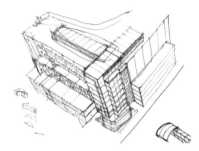

Prebys Cardiovascular Institute

La Jolla, California, USA

383,000 sq. ft. / 35,580 sq. m.

Completion: 2015

The new Prebys Cardiovascular Institute on the campus of Scripps Memorial Hospital is the region's largest and most advanced center dedicated to cardiovascular care.

The seven-story tower unites people and technology in one facility to advance innovative treatment options for patients with cardiovascular diseases.

The contemporary design features an exterior composition of brick, glass and metal panels that respects the aesthetic of campus buildings. Stacked brick and the punched windows that line the north and west facades relate to the La Jolla campus and its architectural character. The curved glass curtain wall on the southeast presents a message of transparency to the community. Glass curtain walls enclose the stairs on the south, east and west facades, serving as beacons of light.

An enriched hardscape of colored concrete pavers extends from the tower's face to the vehicular circulation, echoing the building's concave shape. From this form, a succession of lines is created with trees that extend out from the building.

Interior spaces support advanced medical treatment, patient care, research, clinical trials and graduate medical education within an environment that delivers patient-and-family-centered care. The flexible layout supports the hospital's mission while accommodating future plans for growth.

Large, circular skylights and a well-defined ceiling plane help organize the space, while both the ceiling and floor patterns provide intuitive wayfinding cues. Inspired by the light, colors and textures of the natural landscape and beauty of La Jolla, the interior materials and finishes establish an engaging yet peaceful setting that promotes healing.

The 167-bed institute includes 59 intensive-care beds, four operating rooms, two hybrid operating rooms, six cardiac catheterization labs, diagnostic testing and digital imaging. All patient rooms feature a wall of floor-to-ceiling windows to provide patients, visitors and staff with abundant natural light and expansive views.

The facility represents the first phase of a 25-year master plan that is transforming Scripps Memorial Hospital's La Jolla campus.

◀ view from the southeast

▲ level 5 floor plan

1 public elevator lobby
2 patient elevator lobby
3 waiting room
4 consult room
5 office
6 conference room
7 surgical patient room
8 nurses' station
9 nurses' breakroom
10 storage
11 it support space

▲ site plan

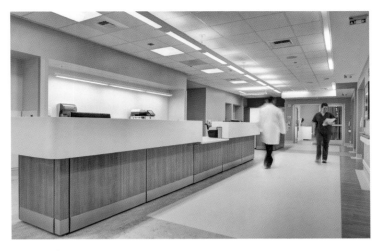

▲ nurses' station

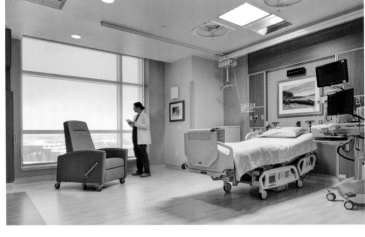

▲ patient room

▲ level 2 corridor

view from northeast

▲ view from south

▲ ambulance entrance

PREBYS CARDIOVASCULAR INSTITUTE

Residential Community for Confidential Corporate Client
Middle East

Residential:
40.3 million sq. ft. / 3.7 million sq.m.

Community amenities:
9.6 million sq. ft. / 895,000 sq.m.

Commercial:
9.5 million sq. ft. / 888,000 sq. m.

Site:
2,580 acres / 1,050 hectares

Completion: 2018

This master plan and conceptual design for a new sustainable housing development creates a self-sufficient, mixed-use community to replace an existing campus for employees of a Middle Eastern company.

The company offers employees a homeownership program that includes a free lot or lot allowance and a subsidized housing loan so that they can build or purchase homes.

Situated on 2,580 acres of vacant land, the pedestrian-oriented development is composed of small communities, each with its own unique identity and located near schools, parks, stores and community amenities.

Balancing the social, economic and environmental needs of its residents, the new development sets a benchmark for livable, walkable and energy-efficient communities in the region.

The master plan includes more than 8,000 residential units. To supplement the homeownership units, the proposed commercial residential development features an additional 2,128 residential units, including 321 villas, 94 townhomes and 1,713 apartments. The plan also incorporates a 200-key, three-star hotel; a 190-key, four-star hotel; a 1.9 million-sq.-ft. retail mall; and an 860,000-sq.-ft. retail souk.

◀ aerial view

▲ commercial + residential properties

1 north compound   5 south gate   8 central core retail
2 boulevard   6 south compound   9 west gate
3 retail mall + hotels 7 central core apartments 10 northwest gate + retail
4 north gate

▲ access + gateways

○ primary gateways   ▬ 22m parkway   ▬ 40m main roads   ▬▬ phasing line
◯ secondary gateways   ▬ 30m main roads   ▬ 60m main roads

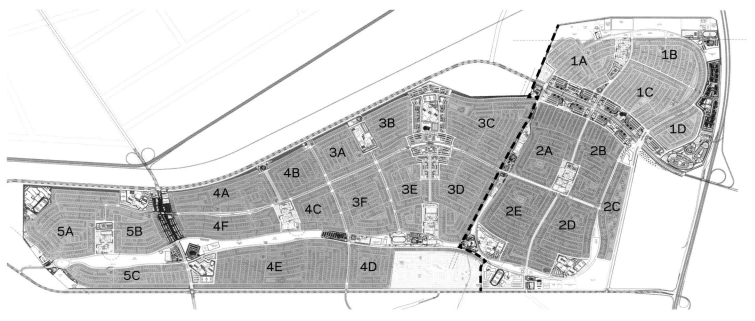

▲ district neighborhoods

░ district 1: 4 neighborhoods   ░ district 4: 6 neighborhoods   ▬ ▬ phasing line

░ district 2: 5 neighborhoods   ░ district 5: 3 neighborhoods

░ district 3: 6 neighborhoods

▲ residential + community buildings

░ green space   ░ recreation centers   ▬ ▬ phasing line

░ housing   ■ facility buildings

░ schools   ░ health facilities

■ mosques

▲ site plan

1	retail mall	5	office buildings
2	retail souk	6	apartment buildings
3	hotels	7	inline retail
4	residential compound	8	gas station

▲ northwest gate retail street

▲ residential compound

▲ mixed-use boulevard

▲ gas station

▲ retail mall

▲ hotel

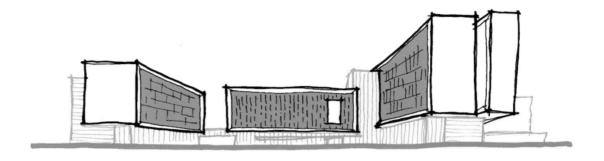

Sidney & Lois Eskenazi Hospital
Indianapolis, Indiana, USA

1.4 million sq. ft. / 130,000 sq. m.

Completion: 2013

This public hospital and medical center creates a contemporary academic healthcare environment that merges clinical, research and educational missions on the campus of Indiana University-Purdue University Indianapolis.

The 37-acre complex replaces the nearby Wishard Hospital, presenting an opportunity for a complete transformation that is rare for urban academic medical centers. Rather than create a massive single structure, the team assembled hospital elements into distinct programs, creating a series of linked buildings and spaces. This thoughtful composition creates open courtyards that complement the rigor of internal spaces.

Structured around a central green space, the medical center includes a 315-bed hospital linked by a two-level concourse to a 275-exam room ambulatory care clinic, a faculty office building, a 2,700-car parking garage, two utility buildings and public plazas.

The facade is defined by a contemporary use of glass, metal and precast concrete panels. These simple, modern materials articulate frames, planes and volumes that define internal functions and communicate a broader community identity about the hospital's programs.

Every aspect of the design focuses on the health and wellness of patients. Reorganizing care delivery for all key departments has streamlined patient movement and eliminated wasted space. The efficient plan enables the new hospital to serve 20 percent more patients in one-third less space.

The public realm framework provides a system of roadways, pathways and landscape between the hospital and the university campus. Positioned at the main entry to the hospital and clinic, The Commonground at Eskenazi Health is a flexible public plaza with water features and a restaurant pavilion.

The Eskenazi Health Sky Farm, a rooftop fruit and vegetable garden with 5,000 square feet of growable space, highlights healthy eating and wellness habits while giving patients and employees opportunities to enjoy nature.

Though the northern climate is challenging and both the hospital and ambulatory care clinic use 100 percent outdoor air, the project is expected to achieve LEED Silver certification.

◀ view from the southeast

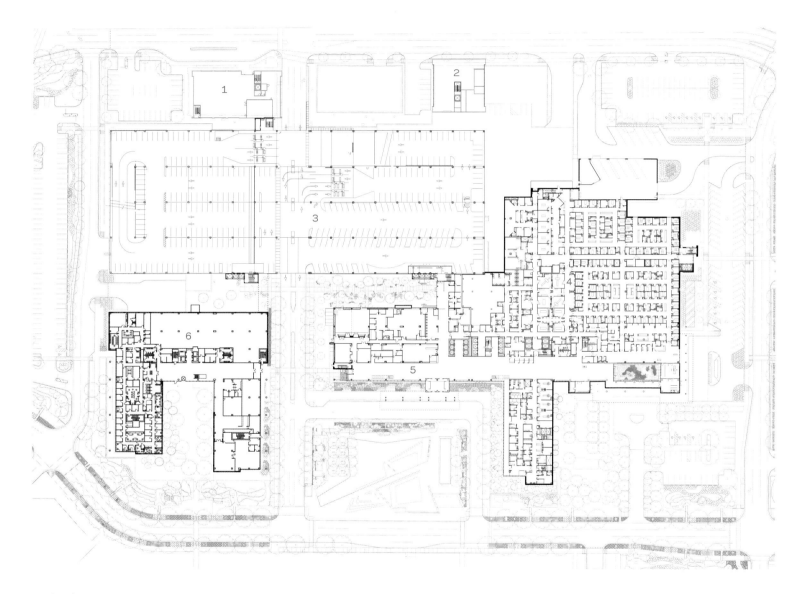

▲ site plan

1 central boiler plant
2 central utility plant
3 parking garage
4 inpatient hospital
5 ambulatory care building
6 faculty office building

▲ main corridor with hanging ceiling sculpture

0 20 40 80 120 200ft

▲ concourse

▼ building cross section

1 faculty office building
2 ambulatory clinic building
3 clinic rooms
4 concourse
5 inpatient hospital
6 helistop
7 facility services
8 surgery
9 emergency room entrance

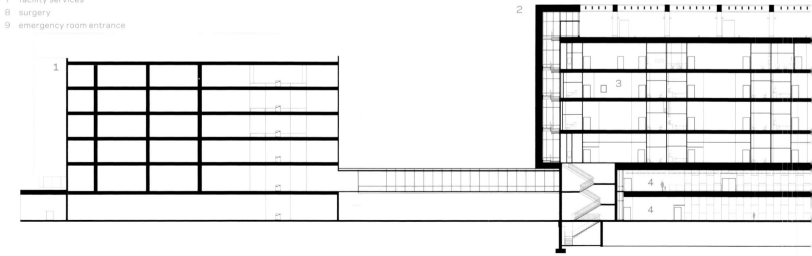

▲ facade sunshading

▲ light patterns at main entrance lobby

▲ eskenazi plaza lighting

▲ eskenazi health trail looking east

▲ parking garage wind veil

St Bartholomew's Hospital Redevelopment and King George V Building
London, UK

New construction:
700,000 sq. ft. / 65,000 sq. m.

Completion: 2016

Skanska Innisfree selected HOK to design the simultaneous redevelopment of St Bartholomew's and The Royal London Hospitals. HOK is leading the architecture, interior design, medical planning and landscape design for the largest hospital redevelopment implemented in the UK under the Private Finance Initiative (PFI) funding scheme.

St Bartholomew's was founded in 1123 and is Britain's oldest hospital. Serving a population of more than three million people, the hospital's new nine-story King George V Building includes the Barts Heart Centre, the UK's largest specialized cardiovascular facility.

Some existing historic buildings on the site were refurbished, conserved and integrated with new construction to create the specialized cancer and cardiac center. The new building, which incorporates the retained King George

V block, features a contemporary design of stone and brick that complements the existing Georgian architecture of London's historic Smithfield area.

Medical professionals at the new Barts Heart Centre will perform more heart surgeries, MRI scans and CT scans than any other facility in the world. State-of-the-art facilities include 10 operating suites, 10 catheterization laboratories, 250 general cardiac beds, 58 critical care beds and 40 coronary care unit beds. Clinicians estimate that more than 1,000 lives could be saved every year because of the state-of-the-art treatment and expanded patient access to a broad range of clinical trials.

The landscape design restores the main square on the site — originally designed by James Gibbs in the 1730s — as a fully

accessible space for patient relaxation. Planting and paving materials enhance the surrounding Grade I and II-listed buildings and historic central fountain that provides a welcome green space in the heart of the hospital.

Part of the redevelopment has achieved an 'Excellent' rating in the NEAT (NHS Environmental Assessment Tool) certification, an independent green building certification method.

The redevelopment has been carried out in phases, enabling the campus to remain operational from the beginning of the project in 2006 through completion in 2016.

◄ central atrium

▲ ground level plan

1 church of st bartholomew-the-less
2 north wing
3 east wing
4 west wing
5 landscaped square
6 entrance
7 king george v building
8 atrium
9 bridge
10 lobby
11 drop-off

▲ st bartholomew's addition

▲ central atrium

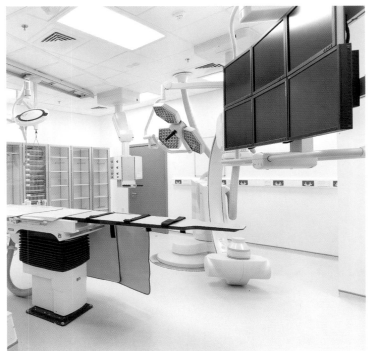

▲ operating room

▲ exterior courtyard

0
5
10
20
40m

Suzhou Times Square
Suzhou, Jiangsu Province, China

99 acres / 40 hectares

Completion: 2009

Times Square is the first international urban mixed-use development in Suzhou. Located in the city's commercial center on the east bank of Jinji Lake, the project integrates retail, dining, entertainment and cultural elements across five districts.

A series of canal-side walkways link the hotels, offices, shopping destinations and open spaces. A sweeping sky canopy features a 1,640-foot-long ETFE (ethylene tetrafluoroethylene) canopy with an integrated LED screen.

The design creates urban landmarks, gateways and plazas to enhance the sense of place and subtly recreate the distinct character of the region's traditional gardens.

Bridges and courtyards establish a rhythm of unique spaces that serve as backdrops and foregrounds for dining, strolling and shopping experiences along the canal.

Visitors access Times Square by water taxi, six subway entrances and 4,000 underground parking spaces. Pedestrian activity flows from the nearby convention center and administrative government offices and from surrounding residences and hotels.

As the cultural heart of Suzhou Industrial Park, the development is integrated with the Suzhou International Expo Center, the Suzhou Industrial Park Administrative Center, and the Suzhou Science and Arts Center. It is designed to serve the needs of the broader region and to support commercial and residential development around Jinji Lake.

◄ view of retail street from under canopy

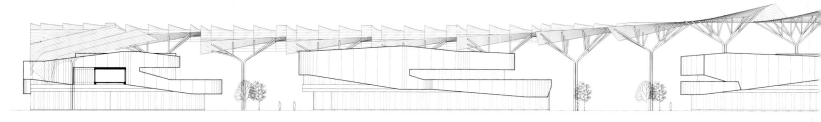

▲ south elevation

▶ site plan

1 office
2 retail street
3 canopy
4 lifestyle retail
5 retail mall

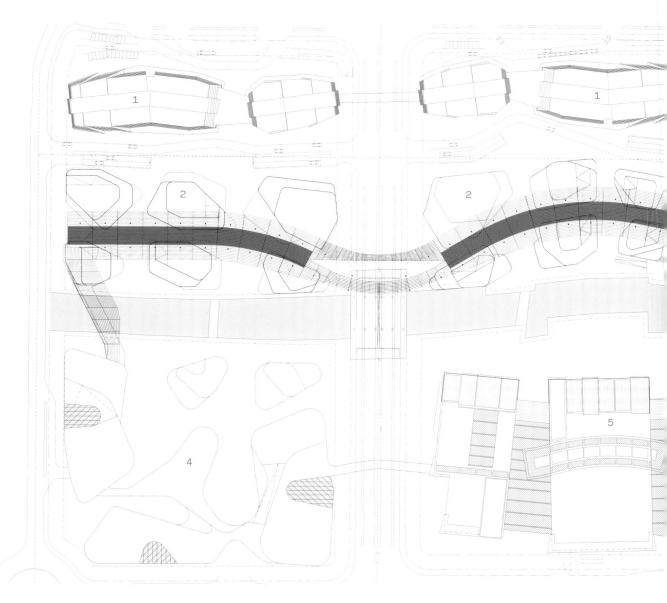

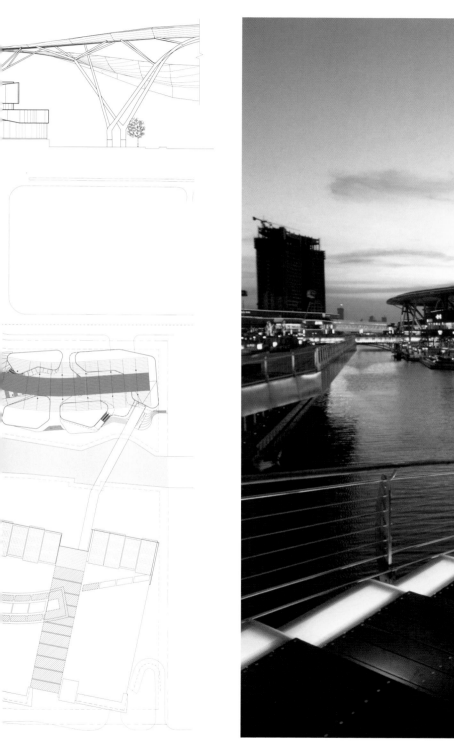

▲ bridge over canal

SUZHOU TIMES SQUARE

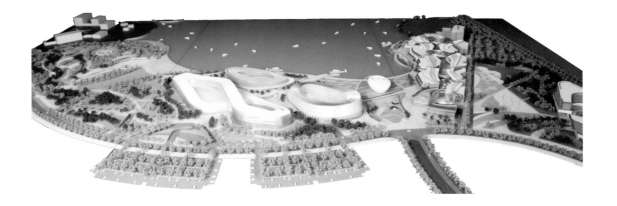

Suzhou Wujiang East Taihu Lake Golden Bay Tourism Complex
Suzhou, Jiangsu Province, China

2.7 million sq. ft. / 252,000 sq. m.

Completion: 2017

This landmark tourist destination on Taihu Lake, the largest lake in eastern China, will introduce ecotourism to China's emerging international and domestic tourism sector.

Taihu Lake is the primary element that organizes all of the development parcels. The north shoreline is urban and supports many activities, while the south shoreline is natural and private, providing more tranquility.

A harbor area to the north and west includes a marina, yacht club hotel and tourist center. The eastern hill area features a water sports park, dry ski slope and visitor center, while the southern delta area incorporates a family hotel and corporate club. All building forms embrace organic shapes to reflect the ebb and flow of the natural environment.

By enhancing the lake's pristine natural environment, the design creates a destination that is commercially viable and ecologically sustainable.

Like a delicately woven fabric, landscaping and new architectural forms trace the Taihu waterfront with an interconnected sequence of public spaces that provide visitors with memorable experiences of exploration and discovery.

A prominent north-south circulation route creates pedestrian paths running parallel to the buildings and along the project's street frontage. Zoning guidelines maximize the building massing along the setback lines. Pedestrian paths divide the built area from the natural softscape.

By leveraging the tidal changes and ecotones of Taihu Lake, the design helps restore wetland areas, protect bird and fish habitats, and improve the lake's water quality. Proposed biological and natural systems will be supplemented by additional mechanical filtering systems.

The project is the first phase of a larger tourism-oriented plan encompassing more than 7.7 square miles along the shores of Taihu Lake.

◄ aerial view from northwest

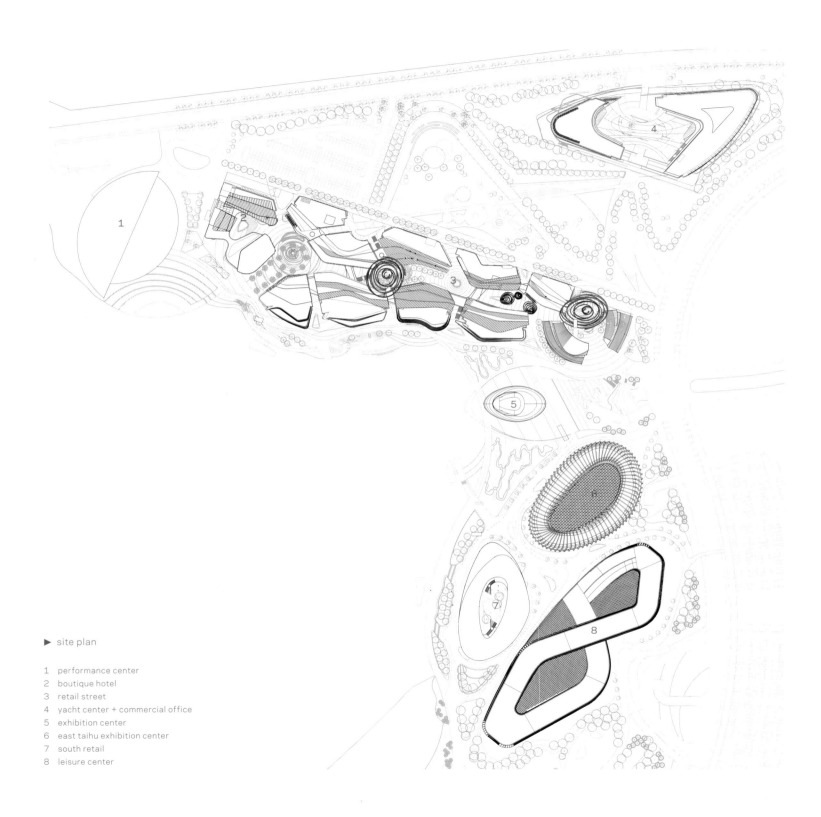

▶ site plan

1   performance center
2   boutique hotel
3   retail street
4   yacht center + commercial office
5   exhibition center
6   east taihu exhibition center
7   south retail
8   leisure center

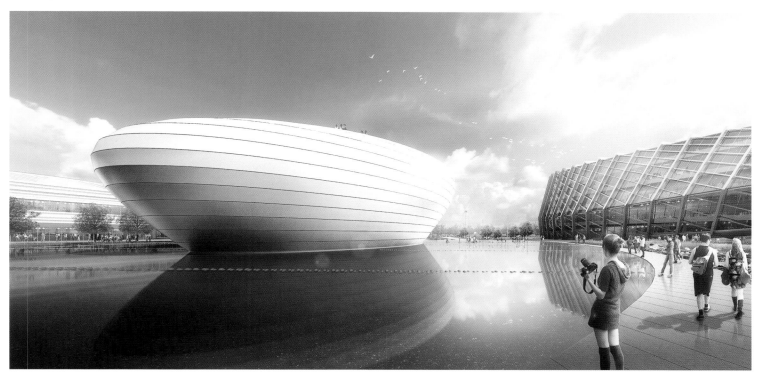

▲ east taihu exhibition center

▲ south retail

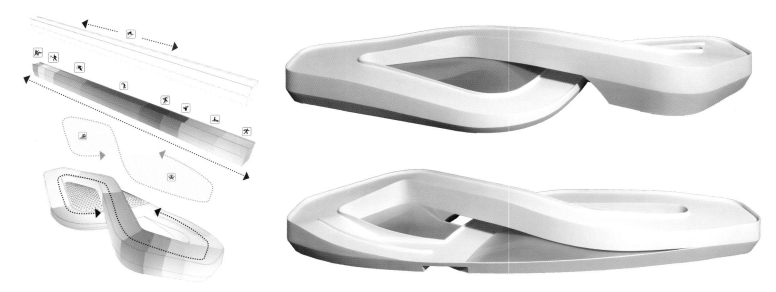

▲ leisure center program organization   ▲ leisure center model

▲ leisure center + park

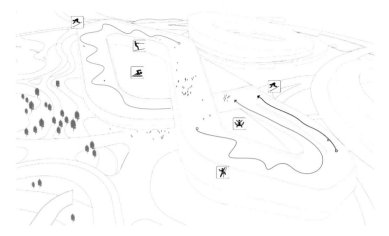

▲ leisure center roof activity diagram

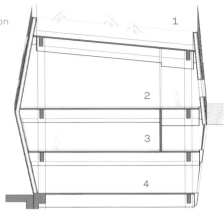

► building use section

1 dry ski
2 sports center
3 gym
4 bowling

► building assembly

1 exterior glazed openings
2 aluminum cladding panel
3 steel + glass triangulated roof
4 curtain wall

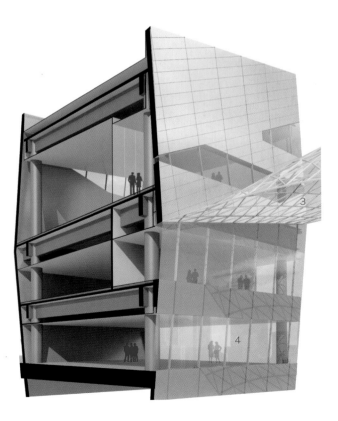

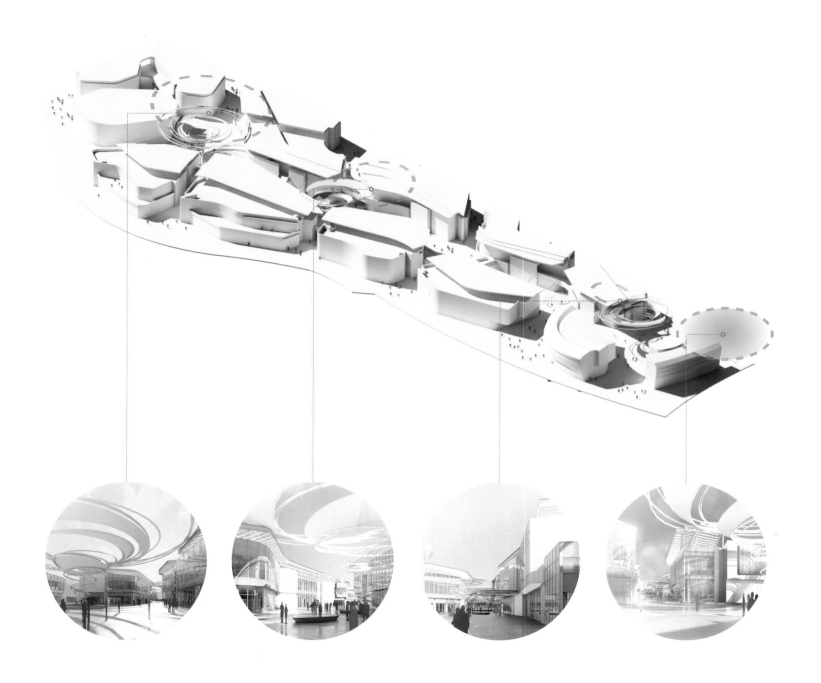

▲ retail street plazas

▲ retail street from the bay

▲ retail street

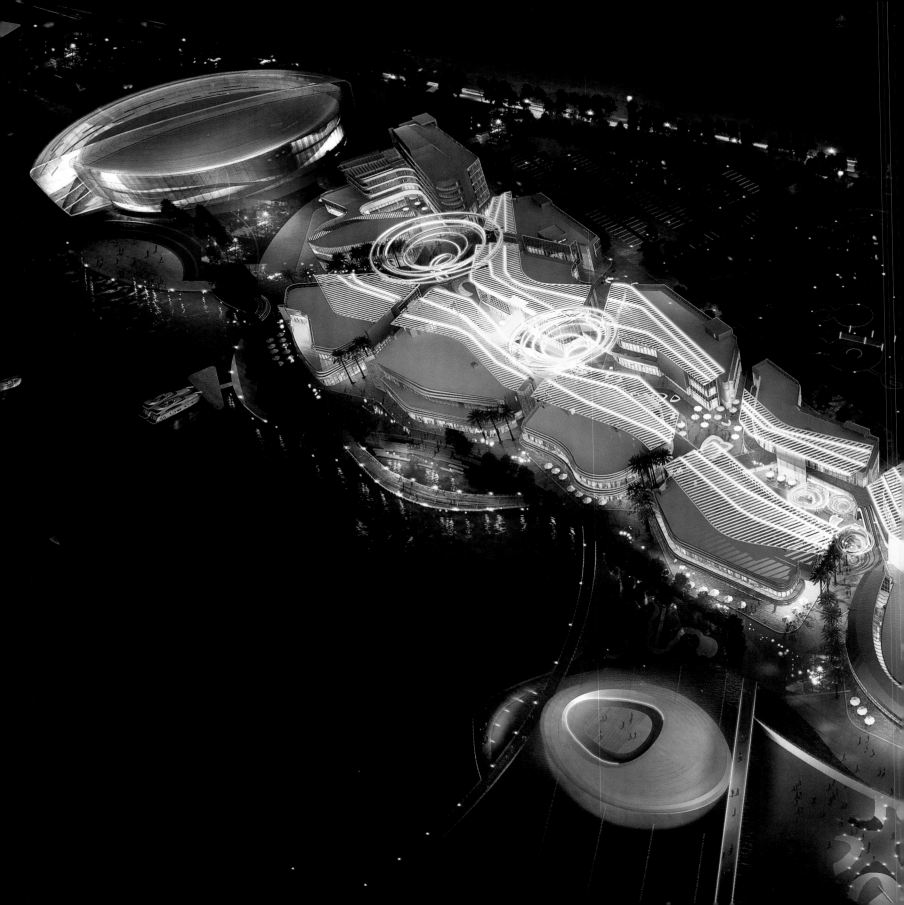

SUZHOU WUJIANG EAST TAIHU LAKE GOLDEN BAY TOURISM COMPLEX

Tower Competition
Dubai, UAE

4.6 million sq. ft. / 427,000 sq. m.

Competition: 2014

This design concept for the world's largest commercial office tower creates a new center of trade and business in Dubai.

Soaring nearly 2,300 feet high, the iconic building forms an elegant, timeless landmark on the skyline. Mixed-use elements at the base are integrated into the tower assembly to create a seamless composition.

The design is conceived as a bundling of three circular tubes with interconnections recalling the diverse intricacies of an ornamental pattern. Slight inward tapers are applied to the building mass near the ground and toward the crown, where each tube is revealed and expressed as a pillar supporting the suspended observation deck.

The tower structure is a dual system consisting of a central reinforced concrete core with mega columns along the exterior that gradually slope to match the facade. The self-shading structure provides passive solar control and energy efficiency. To mitigate wind load challenges, perforated metal "spoilers" or "baffles" along the facade redirect the wind and reduce vortex shedding.

At the base, the building skin becomes a glass drape that provides a dramatic multilevel enclosure for the lower floors and lobbies. The ground plan's circular geometry provides a generous amount of public space and multiple entry points.

The observation deck features a two-level sky hall with a grand space for viewing the city, sea and desert and for hosting special events.

To maximize views, designers clad the building in floor-to-ceiling glass and reduced the number of exterior columns. Use of electrochromic glass minimizes glare and improves energy performance while eliminating the need for exterior shading devices and interior blinds.

The plan organizes the tower into four office zones, each of which functions as a business community with its own lobby and amenities. Elevator cores are arranged around a central hexagon.

An array of lighting effects highlight the building's unique architectural features at night, signaling its presence as a beacon and symbol of strength and aspiration.

◀ view of sky lobby + observation deck

▲ regional site plan

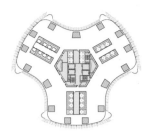

▲ low-rise

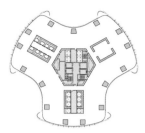

▲ low-mid-rise

▲ sky lobby level 1

▲ sky lobby level 2

► main plaza level

1   entrance
2   tower main lobby
3   retail space
4   retail service space
5   education center
6   cultural center
7   parking entry + exit
8   public plaza
9   terraced fountain

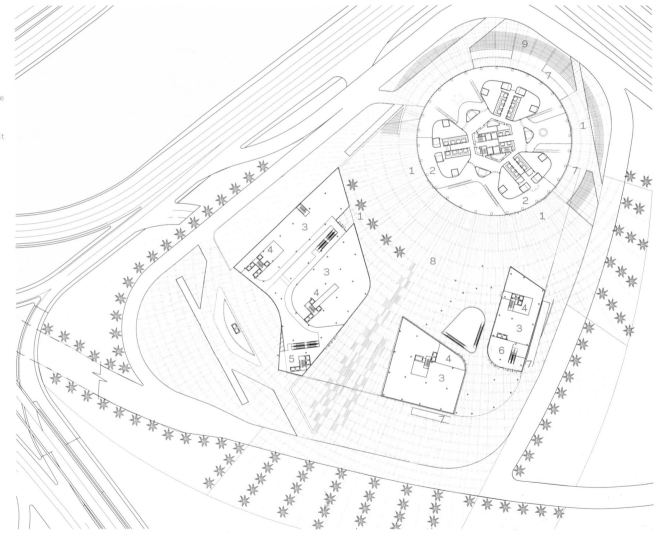

0
10
20

40

60m

299

▶ podium east-west section

1 parking
2 lobby
3 retail
4 hotel
5 event space
6 typical office floor
7 sky lobby

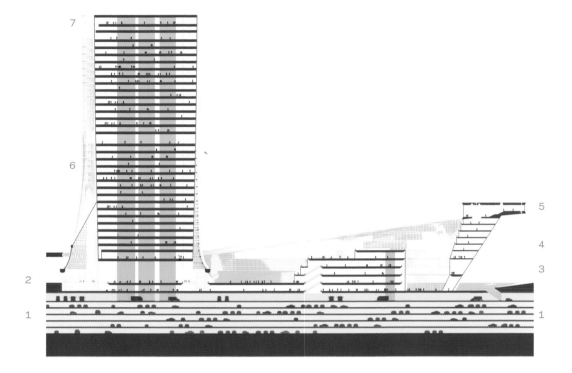

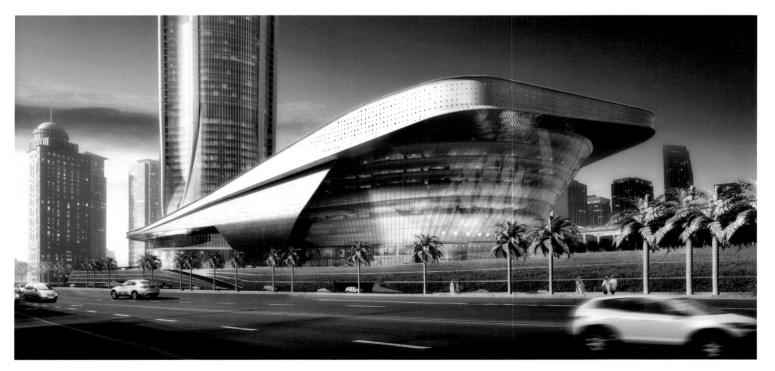

▲ podium view from southeast

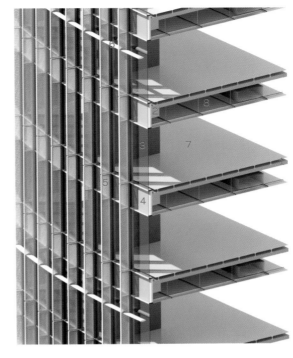

◀ facade assembly

1 concrete deck
2 perimeter beam
3 electrochromic glazing
4 shadow box
5 perforated metal fin
6 horizontal metal fin
7 raised electrical floor
8 suspended ceiling

▲ facade detail

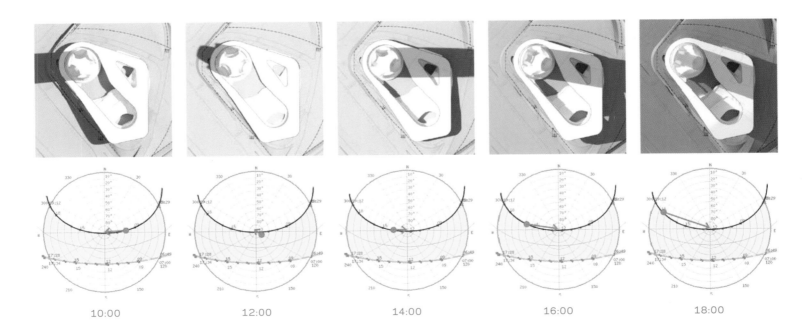

| 10:00 | 12:00 | 14:00 | 16:00 | 18:00 |

▲ sunshading studies